THE
HIDDEN
CONSUMER

Nutrition Facts

3 servings per container
Serving size   **1 cup (180g)**

		Per serving	Per container
Calories		**245**	**735**
		% DV*	% DV*
Total Fat	12g	14% 36g	43%
Saturated Fat	2g	10% 6g	30%
Trans Fat	0g		0g
Cholesterol	8mg	3% 24mg	8%
Sodium	210mg	9% 630mg	27%
Total Carb.	34g	12% 102g	36%
Dietary Fiber	7g	25% 21g	75%
Total Sugars	5g		15g
Incl. Added Sugars	4g	8% 12g	24%
Protein	11g		33g
Vitamin D	4mcg	20% 12mcg	60%
Calcium	210mg	16% 630mg	48%
Iron	3mg	15% 9mg	45%
Potassium	380mg	8% 1140mg	24%

* The % Daily Value (DV) tells you how much a nutrient in a serving of food contributes to a daily diet. 2,000 calories a day is used for general nutrition advice.

uncovering the power of
health-conscious buyers

AMY GRAVES

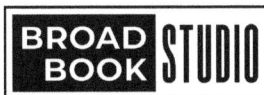

Medical Disclaimer: All material in this book is intended for reference only and should not take the place of medical advice from a licensed practitioner. Please use common sense, do your own research, and consult your physician when making decisions about your health.

Contents

Foreword. v

Introduction: Amy's Journey 7

1 The Hidden Consumer Market: Who Are They? 19

2 Marketing Problems Today. 57

3 Marketing To Hidden Consumers 77

4 Beyond The Food And Beverage Industry 111

5 Completing The Hidden Consumer Journey 139

Acknowledgements 145

About The Author 147

References. 149

Foreword

By Kyle Dine, CEO & Founder of Equal Eats

I'VE LIVED WITH food allergies my entire life. Peanuts, tree nuts, eggs, seafood, mustard—it's quite a list. I've had to read every label, ask every server twice, and sit out more than a few meals while everyone else dug in. It's a routine that's second nature to me now—but it's also a constant reminder that the world wasn't exactly built with people like me in mind.

That's why this book, *The Hidden Consumer*, struck such a chord.

Amy Graves doesn't just tell her story—she shines a light on the daily reality of people who are trying to stay safe in a world that doesn't always recognize or understand their needs. It's personal, honest, and sometimes raw. But it's also a wake-up call to businesses, marketers, health professionals—anyone involved in shaping products and experiences for the public.

While some of Amy's experiences may fall outside what's commonly discussed in medical or industry settings, they reflect the very real frustrations many consumers live with every day. Even if not every detail resonates with everyone, her story is worth listening to—because she's giving voice to challenges that are often felt but rarely spoken aloud.

At Equal Eats, we create tools to help people with allergies, intolerances, and dietary needs communicate clearly—whether they're eating out, traveling, or just trying to live their lives with confidence. We've heard stories from people all over the world who feel left out or ignored by companies, menus, and systems that don't reflect their needs. What Amy describes in this book reflects a real and growing group of consumers—people who read every ingredient, plan every meal, and often feel like no one's listening.

And that's the heart of it: *The Hidden Consumer* is a book about listening. It's about stepping back and realizing that not everyone experiences food—and the world around it—the same way. Whether it's someone managing a non-recognized sensitivity, a chronic health condition, or just trying to shop with a little more intention, these consumers are out there. They're not niche anymore. And they're not going away.

This isn't a clinical guide, and it doesn't try to be. What it offers instead is a powerful perspective on a group of consumers who are often overlooked. It invites us to think differently—about how we label, communicate, and ultimately include people whose needs might not be obvious, but are no less important.

If you work in food, marketing, healthcare, or even policy, this book may challenge you—in ways that are ultimately valuable. It might make you pause or reconsider assumptions. But more than anything, I hope it helps you recognize people you may not have noticed before—and understand how their experiences can inform more thoughtful, inclusive systems.

Introduction: Amy's Journey

I CANNOT BUY FOOD in a grocery store.

In 2013, I began the journey to where I am today. I was having an allergic reaction to food, but it was difficult to pinpoint the cause. I had already narrowed it down to gluten and soy, but there was more involved. The standard allergy tests did not identify the culprit. As I dug deeper, I learned my issues were related to corn and corn derivatives, but I was still reacting to food, despite avoiding these triggers. I had to go further into my research on what I was reacting to and the impact it was having on my body.

I began to understand the depths of the food and packing industries as I went on my journey to discover what food and packaging were making me sick. I also learned how little we, the general population, know about food production of our shelf-stable foods.

When I started noticing I was reacting to food, I saw my allergist and we ran blood work, and I tested negative for food allergies. I was placed on meds to treat eczema. But reactions to food kept recurring, and I was frustrated. Why couldn't I eat without some level of illness? I tested positive for environmental allergies to mold, dust, birch trees, grass, and pet dander. I also began a regimen of allergy shots to help alleviate the symptoms, which I eventually discovered I was allergic to as well. Yes, I was allergic to allergy shots.

But food was a different matter. I had to begin to track what foods caused different reactions. It looked like wheat was the culprit. One night I had prepared spaghetti and 2 bites in I was down with a massive headache. I couldn't find a food tracking journal that tracked the right information for me. So, I created my own journal in a notebook.

I began the process of eliminating gluten, but I was still getting sick. I randomly figured out I was also sensitive to soy when I was getting ready to go to work one day. I was feeling fine and took my supplements. Then boom—immediate headache and nausea with dizziness. Soy had been on my radar, but it was everywhere with gluten. So, when I eliminated gluten, I thought it would be fine. I did not check my supplements ingredients. Why would we check ingredients on something that should be safe? I ended up missing one day of work and learned an important lesson: Check everything you put in your body. The problem was, I did not realize the extent to which that would be necessary.

By 2013, I was in year three of an off-and-on-again sinus infection. My primary doctor was useless. Nothing was working, and I had no idea what to do. I happened to be switching to a different neurologist at the same time. The neurologist, Dr. Masood R. Ghazali, requested an MRI of my brain. We were eliminating Multiple Sclerosis (MS) as a possible cause of pain and temporary paralysis symptoms. On October 24, 2013, I received a call from his office. I did not have MS, but they did find a lump, possibly a cyst, in my nasal cavity. I was told to see my primary doctor ASAP.

I was referred to an Ear, Nose, and Throat specialist (ENT), Dr. Nissim Khabie. In our consultation, he said he would remove the cyst and widen the nasal area inside for better flow. He also noticed that I had a hole in the membrane. The surgery was scheduled for March 2014. It did not go as planned. I had so many pockets of infection in both nasal passages he could only open one side. He focused on removing all the pockets of infection instead. The cyst? A lump of infection.

DETERMINING THE CAUSE

At my first post-op appointment, Dr. Khabie stressed he only sees impacted issues like mine in relation to food allergies. He said I needed to figure out what I was reacting to. During the surgery I kept having an allergic reaction to the sensor pads used on my body. The longest a sensor could stay in one place was five minutes, but this was a two-hour surgery. I woke up with a rash all over my upper body. I had forgotten to tell the team I was allergic to adhesive in patches and Band-Aids. I used, and still do today, gauze and paper tape to wrap cuts.

The process of trying to find my allergen began immediately post-op. By October 2014, it looked like corn was my issue. My reaction to the sensor pads used in surgery was a clue. Corn is used to make glues and the adhesive of sensor pads and Band-Aids. My reaction to the sensor pads in surgery was a clue. But I had other clues that I was seeing and trying to determine what it all meant. Like most people, I did not comprehend that the FDA did not recognize all allergies.

Between March 2014 and October 2014, I started using a notebook as a food journal to document my experiences for my allergist. No food journal on the market could track what I needed to, so I made my own. I tracked each item of food I ate. I tracked the time I ate, what time the reaction started, and what the reaction was. I also tracked all the ingredients in each item I ate. I started seeing some trends, but I still did not know what they meant. I was still taking at face value all the lab-created ingredients, like dextrose, and not looking deeper into the issue. I believed, like so many, that dextrose was "just" sugar. That's what we are told, isn't it?

Between October 2014 and January 2015, I started putting it all together. The reason I started looking at corn was because high fructose corn (HFC) syrup was in the news. HFC syrup was a constant factor in all the foods I was eating to that point. By mid-2015 the FDA granted companies the right to hide HFC under the label "natural flavors," so it no longer appears on food packages.

I began by removing high fructose corn syrup from my diet. The next time I had a migraine, I avoided soda, but I did take my meds. I was down for three more days with a migraine pain so severe I wanted to cut my head off. I had never had so much pain before. When I was on the mend, I checked the ingredients. The issue was the amount of corn used in medicine from HFC to cornstarch.

But I kept reacting to foods with no obvious corn in them. I started doing more research and found the Corn Allergy Girl's Website. What I learned from her was how much corn was in everything. I had no idea how invasive corn was in our diet, products, and clothes. Almost every ingredient made in a lab starts as corn or on moldy corn. On January 21, 2015, I posted this on Facebook: "Here are a couple of WTH (what the hell) moments with a corn allergy: I'm allergic to my allergy meds and paper plates." I literally could not get away from it, and no I was not eating the paper plates. But any food on the plate becomes contaminated. This was the start of me understanding that I was super-sensitive in the world of intolerances and allergies.

To put the sensitivity level of a super-sensitive into perspective, consider someone who avoids gluten to someone with celiac disease. Those who become ill due to gluten don't necessarily need to avoid wheat derivatives. But a person with celiac disease cannot tolerate one-part-per-billion of any gluten or wheat source. In the world of gluten-free, the celiac person is super-sensitive.

THERE'S CORN IN THAT

My journey goes beyond what we believe is safe. The story of what I had to do is what many with unrecognized intolerances and allergies must endure to stay safe and out of the emergency room.

As I realized the extent of my sensitivity, I had to make the decision to reduce food I purchased to only items with five or fewer ingredients. If you look at packaged food with lines of ingredients in ridiculously small font, you will see most are derived from corn. But that wasn't a guarantee either. I also had to look at what those five ingredients were. This led to not only even more food being eliminated, but also everyday household products. The number one culprit? "Natural Flavors." Overall, these ingredients are not natural, and this is where companies can legally hide ingredients they don't want you to know about, like high fructose corn syrup.

My journey educated me on the multitude of ways corn was in my everyday life. I had to get all new cooking utensils and cookware for my kitchen. Anything with a non-stick coating? It used corn starch in the coating and heating it up released particles into my food. Plastic or silicone cooking utensils? Same as the cookware. Plastic dishes? Made from corn, so it had to go. I donated a lot of goods to friends and thrift stores.

But realizing corn was in everything from my face cleansers to makeup to tampons was the ultimate lesson in hidden corn. I cannot use shave creams or gels or a razor with a "moisturizing strip." They all are contaminated by corn. I would shave once a month because the rash was so intense, I could not shave until all the hives and rashes had vanished. Tampons were the worst because I broke out in hives inside my body. I wanted to cry from the pain because corn is used to make most tampons.

In the early 2000's I was diagnosed with exercise-induced asthma. Three years of dealing with a sinus infection had led my doctor to believe that my exercise-induced asthma had become worse. However, as I went through the process of removing corn and other synthetic ingredients from my diet, my asthma went away. On a regular visit to my allergist, they discovered my issue was not asthma but Vocal Cord Dysfunction (VCD), which occurs when the vocal cords do not open correctly. VCD is sometimes confused with asthma because some of the symptoms are similar. According to the American Academy of Allergy, Asthma, and Immunology, "In asthma, the airways (bronchial tubes) tighten, making breathing difficult. With VCD, the vocal cord muscles tighten, which also makes breathing difficult. Unlike asthma, VCD is not an allergic response starting in the immune system." This is why it can be difficult to differentiate between asthma and VCD. Many of the symptoms are similar: difficulty breathing, coughing, wheezing, throat tightness, hoarse voice, and voice changes.

Why did it take so long for a proper diagnosis? My allergy symptoms were always present 24 hours a day/365 days a year with minimal change. As the allergen was removed, my symptoms slowed down or disappeared. We could now see what the actual issue was.

My allergist believed that the constant drip and drainage of mucus down the back of the throat forced my body to find a new way to use my vocal cords resulting in the dysfunction. Based on this and other medical history, it is possible I have been dealing with signs of an allergy to corn and potential corn derivatives since the late 1990's to the early 2000's, which means the asthma diagnosis was wrong from the beginning. Today, I have no asthma symptoms or evidence of asthma.

What happened when corn was removed? Freedom. I could literally breathe again and spend time doing things instead of nursing a headache or migraine. My quality of life is worth everything I had to give up.

One of the fascinating aspects of this journey is how other people who suffer from food-related allergies start to think about their own experiences. As I spoke with them, I could see them putting two-and-two together. It was normal for people to follow up with me and say they also found food to be their issue. In the last few years, I have seen more people sharing their food journeys and struggles related to their allergies.

IMPACT ON THE FAMILY

My husband and I were married in June of 2000. Lee has been by my side through a multitude of doctors' appointments and diagnoses. As one would expect, this was not easy on him either. We had a lot to figure out together to keep me safe but still find a balance so he could eat what he wanted.

Our main meals together were always, and still are, focused on what I can eat safely. If I couldn't eat it, we wouldn't make it. We agreed not to make separate meals for a couple of reasons. One, if we made Lee a meal which I could not eat we would be dealing with cross-contamination in our kitchen. This would put my meal at risk. Two, it seemed silly for each of us to make two separate meals if it was not necessary. This doesn't mean we have only Amy-safe foods in the house. Breakfast and lunch foods for Lee are typically items I cannot eat. In the early days, he might have a peanut butter and jelly sandwich. All of that would make me sick. As he moved towards a healthier snack, he might have pita bread and hummus; again, that would make me sick. His snack items are usually not safe for me either.

We created two areas for food storage: one for me, and one for Lee. In the beginning, we had to have a few discussions about not eating my food. Or even drinking my water when we go out. If he eats my food that means less for me to eat. My food is not easily replaced either. I cannot run to the grocery store and replenish. On the other hand, he can still eat pretty much anything. When he needs food, he runs to the grocery store or even the gas station—but I can't. This is a common problem for the Hidden Consumer. Any safe food and products are not readily available in stores. Many of us need to shop online and order directly from companies.

The ability to make food at home is imperative but also ridden with obstacles. The positive side is we enjoy finding recipes to use for meals. We have become experts at ingredient substitutions and playing with a recipe to find alternatives. Here's an example of ingredients we would use to make a simple steak and potatoes meal in the early days realizing the full extent of my sensitivity.

- **Olive Oil:** purchased at an oilerie in Maple Grove, MN, who imports olive oil and extra virgin olive oil from Italy.
- **Baking Dish:** ceramic with no extra coatings.
- **Steak:** from a rancher in Zumbrota, MN.
- **Potatoes:** from the farmers' market.
- **Herbs:** from our garden and the farmer's market.
- **Salt:** safe sea salt or pink Himalayan salt.

We ate this type of meal for every dinner during the winter months, up to five months out of the year.

I had to learn a new normal for going out of the house as well. When I left home for work, I had to pack a safe meal in safe containers. When we go out, I always have safe water with me. Safe water is tap water from the kitchen (yes this is safer than any water from plastic) in my stainless-steel water bottles or spring water in a glass bottle. Again, Lee can drink any water from anywhere. When he drank my safe water, I had no way of replenishing it until we got home.

At home, I went room-by-room to find all the allergens. I had to determine what was still making me sick. At any given time, you could hear me say things like; 'Why the fuck did they put corn in this?" Or "Seriously, only I would react to something like this!" I was not and am not the only one with these reactions, but my severe sensitivity really made me feel alone in the world of allergies and intolerances. This went beyond food. We had to switch everything from laundry detergents to toilet paper to cookware. We also had to switch to each of us using different products, like toothpaste, hand soap, and even laundry detergent whenever it seemed feasible.

The more I eliminated it, though, the better I felt. And I quickly realized the problem is the rate at which companies are using corn-based ingredients is faster than science can research the effects. It's hard for consumers to keep up, especially Hidden Consumers.

THE MOVE TO CALIFORNIA

The bigger impact on our family was the need to leave Minnesota. On August 1, 2018, my husband and I moved to California for one reason: food. We had vacationed in Paso Robles and surrounding areas for spring break in March of 2018. The amount of fresh food I found, and I didn't have a reaction to, surprised me. My suitcase to travel was filled with supplies from water bottles to rice. We picked a bungalow at the Back Bay Inn so I would have access to a stove to cook my rice. I didn't need as much as I thought I would. I gained 10lbs that week. The week after we were back in Minnesota, I had a meltdown. I cried over not having fresh spinach. Who cries over fresh spinach? Apparently, me. I also lost almost all the weight within the first week back.

I knew I couldn't continue to live in an area where I could not find food year-round. Lee and I talked about moving anywhere I could get food and maybe fresh fish again. I love seafood. He applied and interviewed for jobs up and down both coasts. He eventually received two offers in California. We came to Southern California to look at the schools. He nervously accepted a position at Santiago High School in Corona. We came back in June for Lee to sign paperwork, and I looked for places to live.

This was not an easy move. By this point, Lee and I were both in our 40s. We went from thinking about the future from the perspective of whether we buy a different house within the area to moving across the country. The additional constraint was finding a place I could live in that would not make me sick. So much of a home has corn derivatives in it, from carpet to paint.

On top of that, we had to find a home to rent that was one story, all hardwood or mixed hard surface for floors. No carpet. We had to hope the paint they used was an above-average grade that did not depend heavily on corn. Otherwise, I would be sick the moment I walked in the door.

The surprising part is we did find a home to rent relatively quickly thanks to a friend, Heather Henry. When COVID-19 hit we turned to her again for a much longer and arduous process of finding a home to buy.

In July 2020, we bought a home. It had carpet. After four hours of demo, I was down with a severe headache for 36 hours. It wasn't just the carpet; it was also the highly perfumed floor. It seemed like the previous homeowner spilled a bottle of nasty flowery perfume before moving out. Turns out, it was scented carpet cleaner that was to blame. You could tell by the powder residue left behind on the subfloor. Thankfully, while I was down, Lee and Heather were able to remove all the carpet, so I didn't have to deal with it.

The home was gross when we bought it. Dust, another of my allergens, was years, if not decades, old in almost every room. It also looked like ash from the 2018 Holy Fire had never been cleaned from the walls or windows. We still haven't been able to get our windows clean, but that is partially due to the amount of corn used in most products. I have an airborne reaction to most cleaning products, including bleach. When I cleaned the walls, it looked like I hadn't done anything. It's a good thing I planned on painting every room.

UNEXPECTED BENEFITS OF LIFE IN CALIFORNIA

As we assimilated to life in a new state, we found unexpected benefits. For example, holidays have always been hard for me from a food perspective. The focus is on the food and everyone sitting around the table to eat. I was excluded. There was no food for me. The space they used for prep, cooking utensils, pots, pans, and even the dish detergent would make me sick. No one could make me food. No one wanted to change how they cooked to be safe, and I don't blame them. If the shoe was on the other foot, I don't think I would jump through the hoops either. I went as far as to leave the house while the rest of the family ate, and no one noticed. I was gone for four hours. That was the wake-up call.

One of the most surprising aspects of life here was finding friends who **wanted** to cook for me. They were willing to go the extra mile to ensure the food they cooked was safe. It helped that they cooked mostly the way I did. They had safe cooking utensils, pots, and pans they cook food in. I originally brought my own dish soap, but I don't have to do that anymore. As for the food, we shop at the same spots overall. We do farmer's market runs together on Saturday morning. Not all the time, because they can still shop at grocery stores for their food. We try and plan meals once or twice a month where my husband and I go over and hang out with them and have a meal.

It's a rare gift to a person with allergies to have people in your life who are willing to work with you. I am beyond thankful for the Luschers and their families. Lee and I usually spend at least Christmas Day with them. We have our own Christmas Eve tradition, but on other holidays like Thanksgiving we are usually invited to join them. We don't always but it is nice to know I can go and be able to eat with the rest of the group. They have truly become our extended family.

Another unexpected benefit was being able to take more risks eating out. I still must vet a restaurant to determine if it might be safe for me to dine there. I have been able to refine my allergy information, and my reactions based on it. For example, restaurants that are heavy handed with sauces are not safe. Sauces use a lot of corn and corn-based ingredients. At a minimum, cornstarch is used if not also wheat flour which is almost always cross-contaminated with corn. Vinegar used on salads is also not safe due to corn-contamination. However, California has true farm-to-table restaurants. In Minnesota they say farm-to-table, but extraordinarily little food comes directly from a farm. Out here, restaurants will tell you what farm they work with, and their menu changes based on the season, which is a fantastic sign of being a legitimate farm-to-table establishment.

What I learned through sharing my journey is that there are many people with similar stories. I hear about hidden ingredients others must watch out for and how they determine if the risk is worth the enjoyment of being included. What I learned is that people like me are everywhere. They don't only have food sensitivities. They also have medical issues and other concerns.

WHAT TO EXPECT IN THIS BOOK

Food allergies are nothing new under the sun. There is no new information in this book in regard to what they are or how they operate. What you will find in this book is information about who Hidden Consumers like me are, how to reach them, and what they need from brands to become lifelong customers. In this book, I bring together the big picture of factors of the world around us and how they impact our food, thus determining our buying habits. The Hidden Consumer must be aware of so many elements, whether by choice or due to health. Companies that ignore the Hidden Consumer are leaving money on the table.

Everything I address here was initially brought up in discussions with different Hidden Consumers over the last decade. I used the conversations to launch into more in-depth research to find the truth behind certain claims. The goal was to take the claim and discuss the facts as I could find them based on government regulations, peer-reviewed science, and legal cases.

I deliberately spend a lot of time reviewing labeling and food standards, even European Union standards for comparison, in this book. Consumers may have misconceptions about what certain words mean to them versus what they mean to the manufacturer or the government. If you are a company who wants to increase sales, understanding the viewpoint and problem of the consumer is crucial to offering an effective solution.

I wrote this book by using my personal experience combined with my range of professional expertise. My company brings a unique perspective to the world of marketing for the food and beverage industries because of my lived experiences. You create a quality product, and we will bring you the qualified customers. We want to make sure you are found by the consumers who need your product.

When it comes to how I help my clients market to these groups it's not about discussing all the information listed; it's about understanding the Hidden Consumer mindset. If your product is about being better for the environment, we want to focus on the overall Conscientious Consumer. But if your product is truly Vegan then we want to focus on Vegans and Vegetarians and secondly Plant-Based Consumers. All this knowledge gives Hidden Consumers Consulting better information to accurately create copy and content that connects to each consumer. In turn, this increases each client's ability to increase sales in the long term.

I spent a lot of time using corn as an example in this book, because it is in everything, and I have personal experience with needing to detect all the ways it is hidden. But corn is not exclusively used in making all ingredients. Wheat and corn can be interchangeable in the examples you'll read. Most gluten-free products switch out gluten for corn. For those without corn sensitivity, this is perfect. The goal of using corn as much as I did is to demonstrate that ingredient labels need to be more transparent.

During the writing process (and in my own Hidden Consumer journey), I had to learn how our food is made. I relied on my background as a historian to dig into peer-reviewed resources. I used medical, science, and health journals. I looked at the National Institute of Health, the World Health Organization (WHO), and food safety and regulatory standards with the FDA and US Department of Agriculture (USDA). The research shows that our food is making us sick. Conditions from inflammation and chronic pain to kidney failure are linked to the foods we eat. The number of people under the age of 40 with kidney failure is astronomical. Roughly 37 million people (about twice the population of New York) are in different stages of kidney failure.

These problems have created new target markets, who are currently being ignored by companies. One of these ignored groups is estimated to be leaving a minimum of $19 billion in sales on the table each year. These ignored groups of consumers are how my company, Hidden Consumers Consulting, came into existence. I will also cover why these groups are so important and why they are never going away.

My journey left me jaded and frustrated with the lack of knowledge in the food and beverage industry. I am not one to say, "Here's a problem, you go fix it." I prefer to offer solutions. Hidden Consumer Consulting offers a solution to different problems plaguing the food and beverage industry today. This work is not easy. There are a multitude of regulations that need to be considered. But at the end of the day, the work is worth the payoff for the industry and the consumer.

As you read, think about what food you eat. Do you have constant reactions after eating? Is it time to start tracking what you eat and your reactions to food? One of the many health issues I faced that was caused by food intolerances was IBS and eczema. It blew my mind that taking out my allergen would also remove meds I was taking for treatment. I also learned I was allergic to all medications, so there is also that.

If you are part of the lucky minority who don't suffer any type of illness from food, read this with an open mind. My guess is you have at least two people around you that suffer from food-related illnesses. I hope you can read about my experiences to understand what someone close to you has had to endure.

Let's get started!

The Hidden Consumer Market: Who Are They?

LET'S START with the basics: Who is the Hidden Consumer?

The Hidden Consumer is someone who has a food or material sensitivity that is not recognized formally. For example, corn is not a recognized an allergen anywhere in the world. The European Union (EU) recognizes celery as allergen, but the United States does not. Those who suffer from allergies or food sensitivities that are not government-recognized are Hidden Consumers.

These groups of people are growing in numbers, but no official tracking is being done. Think about all of the people in your life who need to avoid an ingredient. Maybe it's onions or garlic. You might not even realize how often a family member or friend is skipping out on food in order to stay safe. People with these unrecognized sensitivities and allergies are shopping with a different focus. They don't look at labels for calories—they look at the ingredients.

There are five groups of consumers with various levels of education about the food they are eating, or more importantly, that they are eliminating from their diet, as well as other health concerns. The groups are:

- Recognized Intolerances and Allergens
- Unrecognized Intolerances and Allergens
- Health-Related Issues
- Those with Disabilities
- Conscientious Consumers

Let's define each of them briefly here. Later, we'll dig more deeply into each category.

Recognized Intolerances and Allergens

These Hidden Consumers are concerned with allergens that are formally recognized by a government entity as a potential threat. Manufacturers of products that contain these allergens must state when the ingredient is being used. This group doesn't need to be quite as intensely focused on researching allergens, as by law they are well documented by manufacturers. The one example of an exception I can think of is those with dairy allergies. Companies have found new ways to hide dairy in their products. People who are intolerant and allergic are struggling to determine where the dairy is hiding in food.

Unrecognized Intolerances and Allergens

Those with unrecognized allergens and intolerances will be your most educated Hidden Consumer. Their health, and sometimes their life, depends on having a deep knowledge of how food and ingredients are made. For example, as a super sensitive Hidden Consumer, I need to not only know in-depth food production details, but I also need to know how packaging is made and its effects on me. The average person in this group will not be as sensitive to materials and ingredients as I am. The key is their intolerance and allergies are not recognized by the government. So, there is no regulation of the allergen, which means manufacturers of ingredients and products do not have to account for it in our food.

Health-Related Issues

People with health issues are the third group. They have a medical need to alter their diet. This covers everything from chronic inflammation to kidney failure. They may not always realize the extent the food they are eating is hurting their health. You may know people in this group who shop for "sugar-free" items to help control their diabetes. Or they shop for low-sodium foods to help control their high blood pressure.

Diabetics watch for sugars but may not be aware of all the hidden sugars in food. They may also be those who deal with chronic pain and look to eat specialty diets to limit inflammation. Those with disabilities may also fall into this category. Many times, diet can affect their chronic pain levels. For example, my ability to walk can be affected by what I eat. My allergen increases my inflammation, which limits my ability to walk or even use my arms.

Disabilities

Americans with disabilities have become a majority of the population. The Hidden Consumer is not only those with food restrictions but those with mobility limitations. COVID-19 pushed the number of people with disabilities from 50 percent to nearly 60 percent. Even if you can provide safe food for an event, can you guarantee access? Federal regulations regarding the Americans with Disabilities Act (ADA) only go so far, and most of us still struggle to not only get into buildings but to maneuver around the facility. If you make a product, is it disability friendly? Are you clearly disclosing your ingredients and is it accessible to all your ideal clients?

Conscientious Consumers

This group includes those who eat based on principles and ethics. This group cares about the welfare of animals and may be vegan or vegetarian. Some may care about the environmental impact of factory farms and the production of processed and ultra-processed foods. They may be moms who want their kids to eat healthier and look for food with specific certifications. Those who wish to eat whole foods and those who favor plant-based lifestyles also fall into this category.

What all these people have in common is a level of understanding around deception in the food industry. All Hidden Consumers want to eat better and to be safe. Whether they have food issues themselves or see food production destroying the environment and as cruelty to animals, they all want to know the companies they buy from understand value goes beyond profits.

Why are there people considered hidden in the world of capitalism? Allergies and intolerances are wide and diverse, and a majority of these sensitivities are not recognized. To understand why, we need to start by understanding the differences in allergies and intolerances.

UNDERSTANDING ALLERGIES AND INTOLERANCES

On my journey, I learned that what the general public, including food suppliers and manufacturers, thinks about allergies and intolerances is outdated or flat-out wrong. Like so many areas of public knowledge, what we think is correct is not 100-percent accurate. For example, many people believe allergens are only those recognized by the government. They accept peanuts as an allergy but believe corn can't be an allergen because there is no federal recognition of it. Let's start by making sure we are all on the same page regarding the differences between allergies and intolerances.

According to the Asthma and Allergy Foundation of America, more than 100 million people in the US experience various types of allergies. This equates to 1 in 3 adults and 1 in 4 children having some level of allergies. To be clear, these are only the people who have an allergy recognized by the government. People like me, who are sensitive to corn, are not included in these numbers.

In the world of allergies and intolerances, there are various levels just like there are different reactions. Allergies and intolerances can be difficult to distinguish between. The main difference is that an allergic response will be life threatening while intolerance can make you unbelievably ill. It's common for a person's reaction to food to be confused with environmental allergies, a cold, or flu, or "just some bug." Quick hint: If you need a box of Kleenex next to you when you are eating ... you are probably reacting to your food.

The food and beverage industries need to understand this information if they want to increase their sales. By understanding the levels of reactions people can have to an ingredient, they can provide better training for customer service and overall communication with all consumers.

It's not easy to tell the difference between reacting to food and colds or other illnesses. It can be downright hard. I did not even realize the connection between what I thought was a "cold" and a "sinus infection" or my environmental allergies flaring up until I started reading my Facebook memories after I discovered the issues.

After I realized I was reacting to corn, I started connecting seeing all of the "I am sick again" posts to my food sensitivities. A great example is from March 12, 2014. Here's what I wrote: "Post op appointment went well today. I'm healing faster than expected but my nerves in my sinus cavity are super sensitive. We discovered the issue when removing the stints and vacuuming out the blood. Four rounds of numbing agents and I still had pain. Next appointment in three weeks." Corn is used in all medications (see my resource guide for more information). In numbing agents, it can be found in corn-based alcohol. Whatever the reason, my body always bleeds more when numbing agents are used. My dentist was the last one to discover this issue. In 2022, I had to have my first crown put on. The dentist and the hygienist could not stop the constant flow of blood from around the injection site while trying to prep the tooth for the model and eventual crown.

My sensitivities are intense, while others' may not be. The key here is to understand how sensitivities vary. Intolerance versus anaphylaxis versus oral allergies have different levels of reaction. Please remember that when someone is intolerant of an ingredient or material, it can still make them sick for days. Many of my reactions to the ingredients I am intolerant to still induce a migraine which no meds will knock out. If I ingest the ingredients, I am intolerant to run the risk of not being able to function for a minimum of 36 hours.

The first thing to know is there are different levels of tolerance. They range from light to super sensitive. I learned about the different levels of tolerance in my different communities, specifically the corn allergy community:

- **Lite.** People in this category don't generally react to derivatives. They need to stop eating the actual ingredient. An example of this would be corn-based ingredients like cornstarch or corn itself. They can still safely buy food in the grocery store. This group can still take most medications, like Benadryl or use EpiPens.
- **Moderate.** These people can tolerate some derivatives. They don't have to cut them all out. They do have to be more careful with what they can eat. This group can still buy food at a grocery store with caution. They most likely have their safe foods they can buy and take precautions when trying new foods. This group will mostly be able to take Benadryl or use EpiPens depending on derivatives they react to. They may also have their medications compounded, if they are lucky enough to have a doctor who understands.
- **Super Sensitive.** Then there are the Super Sensitives. I like to say those of us in this group have the superpower of detecting our intolerances and allergens in any food or product. However, that also makes them our kryptonite. We are the canary in the coal mines according to my allergist. We cannot tolerate the Food and Drug Administration (FDA) "acceptable levels" of our allergen, intolerance or mold in our food or drinks. This also means we don't fit the mainstream thought process of "processing out proteins" to eliminate an allergic response. The FDA acceptable levels refer to processing out a certain recognized allergen; since those levels are still too high it does not apply to those in this category. This group cannot use medications. Even something as simple as Benadryl or an EpiPen will accelerate an allergic reaction response.

The reaction response due to an intolerance or allergy for each group will vary depending on their autoimmune system. All our responses generally fall into known allergic reactions. However, there are other side effects we might also be dealing with on top of the allergic response which show we are also intolerant to certain ingredients.

Anaphylaxis and Other Symptoms

If you are reading this wondering how to tell if your "cold" could be a reaction to food, you need to know what to look for. One of the many things I have learned on this journey is the depth of symptoms one can have as an allergy response. It seems we are taught the only symptom is the closing of the airways. But your body's response to some allergens, or intolerances, can be confused with the common cold, or in my early days, a sinus infection.

I am not a medical professional. If you are experiencing symptoms and are concerned, see your doctor to start a discussion on the next steps. The American Academy of Allergies, Asthma, and Immunology (AAAA&I) has a great list of anaphylaxis symptoms. Notice that many of the anaphylaxis symptoms do not lead to instant death.

The key differences in intolerances and allergies are the outcome of the issue. Both can have similar reaction times starting typically within 5 to 30 minutes. There are some derivatives that affect me with only one sip of a beverage or one bite of food. I will have an instant headache. Sometimes, I don't know if I ingested something I should not have until up to 10 hours later. This is part of why diagnosing the corn sensitivity was difficult. But if it is anaphylaxis, you would see a reaction within an hour or two. It would not be the next day.

Other key similarities are the warning signs of a reaction. Think about your symptoms. If they happen while or after you eat, you could be experiencing a reaction to what you just ingested or breathed in. In my case, I dealt with a wide range of full-body symptoms:

- Rashes and hives. These were a normal part of my life. My skin always had itchy red welts on it all over my body. The worst ones on my body were usually on my arms and hands.
- Swelling of my limbs and abdomen. I did not realize how swollen I was until I removed the corn allergen. I do wonder how much of my weight was swelling versus fat.
- Wheezing. This is what made my doctors believe my exercise-induced asthma had become something more aggressive and required more than rescuer inhalers.

- Passing out. I believe my chronic pain combined with my allergic reaction would lead to severe abdominal pain and passing out in extreme situations.
- Chest tightness, another symptom that led to the asthma diagnosis but compounded by the amount of mucus in my body.
- Trouble breathing and coughing. This was also a consistent issue for me. Even today, some of my initial symptoms that I typically don't notice are stuffy nose and coughing. These are easy symptoms to pass off, believing you have a cold.
- Hoarse voice. I always seemed to have a frog in my throat and no amount of clearing it would seem to make it better. I also had to deal with tingling in the back of my throat.
- Vomiting and, of course, nausea as the precursor. If I ingest actual corn kernels my body will only throw them up. It's like they have the go straight to jail and do not pass go card from Monopoly and are not allowed to pass through the system.
- Diarrhea or intestinal issues (similar to IBS). Gut bacteria is one thing but a body ridding itself of what it sees as a toxin is quite another. At least I was almost always home so I could run to the bathroom as necessary.
- Stomach cramping. I still deal with this, but thankfully not as frequently. The sudden intestinal pain that leaves you holding your stomach and rocking yourself due to the level of pain you are enduring is hard to forget. I believe corn has damaged my body in ways I did not know were possible.
- The pale or red color to the face and body I did not realize was a symptom of allergies. I noticed it but never put two-and-two together until I removed my allergens. I typically develop the red color where my chest and neck meet. My husband now notices it and will comment on it. At this point I usually do not have any other noticeable symptoms.
- Feelings of impending doom. This is not a normal symptom for me, but I have experienced it.

Beyond this list, I also experienced a host of other symptoms. These symptoms are considered more in relation to having an intolerance. My environmental allergies affect how my body reacts to different ingredients. Corn is technically classified as grass. Moldy corn is how most hidden sugars are created. This means my reactions vary depending on what form of corn an ingredient is derived from. Since blood tests do not test for corn, we cannot pinpoint the exact corn chemical that is causing my reactions. Some of my additional symptoms included:

- Eye allergies from my allergen being airborne. My symptoms included watery eyes, itchiness, redness, eyelid swelling, and massive amounts of mucus coming out of my eyes. This mucus was in large enough quantities to seal my eyelids shut.
- Sinusitis. This one is I am sure obvious to most of you given my story about the constant sinus infection. My symptoms were coughing, congestion, postnasal dripping, and toothaches.
- Sinus pressure due to mucus. If my headache is due to being "corned," I get what I call a mucus ball deep in my sinus cavity. The headache and sinus pressure go away once the mucus ball drops. The gross part is it drops straight down into the stomach. The ENT I worked with widened one side of my nostril, so mucus can move quickly down.
- Oral allergies causing tingling in the mouth and on the tongue. My gums would bleed when I put corn-based products in my mouth, anything including toothpaste. I was also dealing with extreme tooth sensitivity. To this day, I still struggle with bleeding gums and sensitive teeth if I eat food bought at a grocery store.
- Migraines that had increased in duration and intensity.
- Headaches with bloody ears. If I eat something contaminated with corn or corn derivatives and end up going down with a headache or even a migraine, I need to clean the dried blood out of my ears the next day.
- Airborne reactions. I deal with these on a regular basis. I have not been to a movie theater since 2014. Popcorn is literally popped corn. Everyone I have talked to about this is shocked when they think about what popcorn is. The reality for me is I cannot be in

a room or building with fresh corn popping. I also cannot be in a building with corn being cooked inside. I will have the same reaction. Reactions I deal with are runny eyes with mucus sealing my eyelids shut combined with persistent coughing and sneezing and tingling in the back of my throat.

- Acne. What I thought was acne turned out to be a reaction to my facial cleansing system and makeup. My face cleared up once I stopped using standard beauty cleansers and makeup. I also had this issue plus rashes, and hives on my scalp and my back due to contaminated shampoo, conditioner, and hair care products.

- Weird reactions like hair loss (which stopped when I removed corn from the diet). The other one was constantly being cold. My body doesn't do a great job of producing body heat (my thyroid has been checked and is normal). Even today when the daily temperature drops below 65 degrees, I have to drink hot water to maintain a comfortable temperature and not freeze to my core.

- Constantly sneezing. I am now in tune to my body enough that if I take a bite of food or have a sip of a drink and sneeze immediately, I know it has my allergen in it.

- Bloating, the constant feeling that my abdomen was bigger or constantly feeling like I had eaten too much.

- Menstrual changes. The worse my other allergy symptoms were, the worse my menstrual symptoms became. I would be down for three days with a severe headache or migraine every month. My cycle would last eight days on average and be heavy for most of it. I could fill a super tampon in three hours. Pads would need to be changed every hour to every other hour. On top of that, the clotting was excessive, and my doctor was concerned about the size of the clots.

I share this to help others who may not realize they are reacting to food; but to also educate the industry. The research that came out in the fourth quarter of 2022 confirms my reactions as related to food ingredients created in a lab. Science is finally catching up with what people have been saying and experiencing for the last few decades. As more people become sensitive to how our ingredients are made, the bigger the problem will become.

RECOGNIZED ALLERGIES AND INTOLERANCES

The first of the five groups of Hidden Consumers are those with Recognized Allergies and Intolerances. This group is what comes to mind for people when they hear "allergies" or "intolerances." The FDA has a list of nine ingredients they recognize as something people could have a reaction to when ingested or encountered. The FDA "major food allergen" list includes milk, egg, fish, crustacean shellfish, tree nuts, wheat, peanuts, soybeans, and sesame.

My favorite group for research on the buying power of the Hidden Consumer is FARE, Food Allergy Research and Education. The data FARE provides have prompted me to niche into this segment of marketing because of my own journey and seeing the full potential of what transparency can do. The downside is their numbers only reflect those with recognized allergies (the Hidden Consumers in this category). Their numbers are truly minimum numbers. If you consider the number of people with allergies who are not recognized, you can start to see the true depth of this group's buying power.

As of September 17, 2023, there are 85 million people avoiding purchasing based on the top nine allergens. In the past 20 years those with recognized food allergies have grown by 4 percent. These consumers spend $19 billion a year and will spend 3-5 minutes reading **one** label. They will also spend up to 5 percent more on groceries.[1]

Here's a quote from the FARE website:

"Back at the beginning, I sold a lot of my belongings along with receiving food stamps and WIC just to afford food, as you can't use food banks when you have allergies. They think it's a luxury. For us, it's life."
Food Allergy Mom

This mom hits the proverbial nail on the head. When I realized the extent of my sensitivity, my husband and I were living on $300 a month after paying our bills. I went to bed every night with my stomach growling and aching due to a lack of food. Eventually, my body adjusted to the limited amount of nutrition and food intake, but it also pushed the move to California. One issue I encountered when shopping was "allergy-free" brands.

Brands cannot call their products "allergy-free." It is not possible to be 100 percent allergen-free. There will always be someone who could potentially have an allergic reaction and will take you to court over it.

The downfall of the brand known as Enjoy Life is a great example of this. Once the FDA recognized sesame as an allergen, Enjoy Life could no longer call themselves allergy safe. So, it was not a shock to me to see Enjoy Life crumble with a new allergen added to the recognized list.

A $19 Billion Underserved Market

The topic of reaching the allergy-based shopper is not new. The problem is finding or creating a good solution that can benefit both business and consumer. In November 2020, the *Progressive Grocer* discussed the biggest impacts the food and beverage industry could have for 2021. "One of the biggest opportunities for the food and beverage industry to serve shoppers in 2021 is to build trust and loyalty with those impacted by food allergies."

The article goes on to cite multiple sources indicating 25 percent of the population in the United States actively avoid food due to intolerances or allergies. They also go on to cite that around 25 million people are directly impacted by allergies. The distinction they *don't* make is it relates only to the population who have FDA recognized allergies. We cannot put an accurate number on how many people have food allergies from ingredient sources not recognized by the FDA because that data is not tracked.

Our perspective is simple. We are not asking companies to be allergy-free or allergen-friendly. What we do is work with clients who want to be transparent in their ingredient list. We have the tools and skillset to market your product to find people who have allergies recognized and not recognized by government agencies. You cannot sell to everyone, but you can cast a wider net to find more ideal clients.

UNRECOGNIZED ALLERGIES AND INTOLERANCES

The second of the five groups of Hidden Consumers is the Unrecognized Allergies and Intolerances. The biggest issue facing this group is their allergies and intolerances are not recognized by the FDA. The ingredient they struggle to avoid is not "processed out" because it is not required. It is also not a requirement for companies to understand how the ingredients in their products are made. To be clear, I am not proposing all ingredients be recognized as allergens. Our solution is for companies to clearly state how ingredients are made and to stop hiding ingredients under the "natural flavors" line. You can use "natural flavors" on a package, but you need to clearly communicate elsewhere what is in this grouping of ingredients.

If we take this a step further and look at the EU, they also do not recognize all allergens and intolerances. But they do recognize five more than the FDA does.[2] The EU's list of "major food allergens" includes: cereals containing gluten—wheat, such as spelt, Khorasan wheat, rye, barley, oats; crustaceans, eggs, fish, peanuts, soybeans, milk; nuts such as almonds, hazelnuts, walnuts, cashews, pecan nuts, Brazil nuts, pistachio nuts, macadamia/Queensland nuts; celery, mustard, sesame seeds, sulfur dioxide and sulfites, lupin; and mollusks such as mussels, oysters, squid, snails. This list is more detailed than our own here in the US. What the EU considers a gluten risk includes a wide range of grains that the US does not include in their own definition of what "gluten-free" means.

The Unrecognized group struggles the most with staying safe. Not everyone can do the research needed to understand their allergen or intolerance. Nor can everyone afford safer foods. I am privileged in being able to move across the country to where I can shop from certified organic farmers markets. But many people do not get that opportunity. Maybe your friend who is **always** sick is struggling with eating safely. It's heartbreaking to see the posts in various groups of people who must eat food they know is making them sick because they don't have the money to do otherwise. Their choice is eating healthy food and having nowhere to live or being sick with a roof over their head.

This group knows you cannot trust the customer service team at the company to know the answers. Often, they give a blanket statement "Our food is safe for you," which may then lead to numerous ER visits. This group of consumers cannot depend on companies to know the base ingredients used to make the ingredients in their products. This also makes this group the most likely to distrust most companies and their marketing claims.

HEALTH ISSUES AND RISKS

Let's get to know more about the Hidden Consumer who is focused on health issues and risks. Our healthcare system is based on keeping us sick. Take a pill to mask the symptoms and don't worry about the cause of the issue. This keeps Americans going back for more pills to cover more symptoms. We all know it. Almost all of us joke about it. Think about the commercials for whatever the latest drug on the market is and the legal disclaimers of all the problems and additional health risks you may encounter because of the medication. I joked with my husband recently about a medication that said a side effect could be the loss of a lower limb! We joke that medicine makes us sick, yet we keep going back for more.

This world of keeping us sick has created a new type of consumer with mass buying power: the consumers who shop based on health issues. This group struggles to find all the hidden ingredients that continue to make them sick.

Finding a doctor who helps you solve the root problem in your body by looking at food and diet first can be nearly impossible. There are people who absolutely need to be prescribed medications. However, the research shows that a number of people on medications for health issues could be struggling because it is the food they are eating that is the root of the problem.

There are people who need to be on medication immediately to get numbers under control. In 2022, my husband Lee also joined the ranks of Hidden Consumers. He was dealing with high cholesterol levels, to which he is also genetically disposed. The doctor prescribed him the medication, but Lee wanted to talk to someone who he thought would understand food and high cholesterol: a nutritionist.

The problem was that the nutritionist was not prepared to deal with someone with Lee's knowledge of food. The nutritionist told my husband to "add more nuts" into his diet and look at the Mediterranean diet, which was not extremely helpful. My husband did the research to determine his best options. He went with a combination of diet and exercise to get his levels to an acceptable range. He's on the lowest dose possible for the medication because of the extra work he puts in to solve the issue. The key is he still needs medication but in conjunction with a healthy diet and exercise, he doesn't need as much.

Another example is from one of my network connections. He is a real estate agent in the Washington, D.C. area. We happened to have a meeting a few months after he was diagnosed with diabetes. The doctor had gone over what ingredients to avoid, but it turned out it was not a complete list.

After his diagnosis he went grocery shopping to buy safe food that did not have sugar. He was excited to find so many products labeled "sugar-free." When he went back to the doctor for his first set of labs after the diagnosis, he found out his levels were three times higher than before. The doctor told my friend he would have been better off eating a tablespoon of sugar everyday instead of eating foods labeled "sugar-free." You cannot trust the food and beverage industry to accurately label their products.

This group of consumers is researching and determining what is safe for them. Their biggest obstacle is lack of ingredient disclosure in the food industry for consumers to make safe choices. If you had to decide whether to try a new food, which could potentially kill you, would you do it? Unless you are comfortable with death, you most likely are not going to try a new food. All this research and looking for answers is also leading to this consumer to be more educated about the foods they buy. For this group in particular, two major food concerns are front of mind: processed foods and proper labeling of organic foods.

Processed and Ultra-Processed

According to research in the *American Journal of Clinical Nutrition*, 60 percent of calories consumed in America came from ultra-processed foods. What are ultra-processed foods? These are foods that are made mostly from substances extracted from foods with added fats, sugars, salts, starches, and hydrogenated fats. Examples of these foods are soft drinks, frozen meals, hot dogs, cold cuts, fast food, packaged cookies, cakes, and salty snacks. As an example: a minimally processed food is corn. A commonly processed food is canned corn. An ultra-processed food is corn chips.

The research shows the biggest problem with our food is processed and ultra-processed foods. What I can tell you is based on what I had to learn to keep myself safe, the root issue is these foods are made in a lab and contain highly refined ingredients. From a personal perspective, I also find it telling that all the ingredients listed in the research are derived from corn. What we are learning is the extent to which the problem is affecting Americans. Our rise in chronic conditions, obesity, kidney failure, and heart attacks can often be traced back to these foods.

According to an article in *Scientific American* by Lori Youmshajekian, the stats are high. Adults consume nearly 60 percent of their calories every day from ultra processed foods. In children and teenagers, this jumps to 70 percent every day. The concern is that the number of calories we consume that are considered processed or ultra processed are leading factors in our declining health.[3]

The most recent published research came out February 2024 in *The BMJ*. This study found that ultra-processed food was directly associated with 71 percent of health parameters. These included mortality, cancer, mental, respiratory, cardiovascular, gastrointestinal, and metabolic health outcomes.[4]

When I have discussions with companies about how their ingredients are made, most are unaware. Their general focus is on acquiring ingredients with the lowest price to increase their profit margin. It makes business sense to do this, but how they communicate their ingredients will be a key factor in their future success.

A great example is a winery I worked with in the early days of my corn diagnosis. My husband and I were talking to the winery owner and apologizing for having to drop our membership to the wine club. Their wines consistently made me sick. Based on my knowledge of wine making, which was not extensive at that time, I had determined the sugar used was the culprit. When we were discussing this, the owner took offense as most people do. They said there was no way corn was in their sugar. They were related to the salesman, and he would not sell a subpar product. It turned out, I was right. They did two things after that. One, they switched their sugar for winemaking. Two they researched all their other ingredients and discovered that they were using products they were not proud to support. They changed their process to be informed on how the ingredients in their wine were made and started the process of becoming Vegan Certified. Their commitment to vetting the ingredients led to working with local vegan restaurants and shops and expanding their wine business.

The flip side is most food companies do not understand how untrustworthy they are because of their lack of knowledge. From the C-level down to customer service, what is said to those with allergies could be deadly. Think about those with celiac's disease. They generally cannot eat gluten-free products processed in the United States. The level of gluten the FDA allows in American food is higher than the standards in the EU. Since the EU lists more varieties of wheat and grains that are considered allergens. Those with celiac's disease may have an easier time eating in EU countries than at home. The EU is not perfect. But they do a few things better towards transparency.

I have a few friends with various levels of intolerance from gluten-intolerance to celiacs. A few of these friends have traveled to Italy and discovered they could eat safely and enjoy most foods. Back in the States they had to go back to avoiding almost all if not all wheat-based foods. While not scientific, it is a common story I hear. If the restaurants and bakeries in Italy used my method of transparency, they would be able to reach more tourist business plus local business. Allergies and health issues are a world-wide phenomenon. It is not limited to only Americans. If Italy, as an example, had more disclosure around ingredients used, it would encourage more tourist dollars to be spent. More tourists would feel comfortable purchasing goods and have less stress. If more tourists are relaxed, happy, and stress-free, the more likely they are to spend money.

It will take another book to delve into the economics of America and the food industry but suffice it to say, the average American cannot always afford fresh food. This means we often buy the food that we can afford. The cheapest food on the market is processed and ultra-processed. Bioengineered food is also moving into this category.

If you have health issues or food allergies, you cannot always trust government regulations to keep you safe. First, the amount of mold and food defects allowed in your food could be dangerous when in combination with mold in ultra-processed and processed foods. The FDA, according to its food safety training and certification guidelines, allows a certain amount of mold and defects to be present in your food based on the product. An example of a product defect is canned sweet corn. The FDA allows 2 or

3 mm or longer larvae, cast skins, larval or cast skin fragments in the aggregate length of insects or insect parts exceeds 12 mm in 24 pounds.

Our food when produced or created in processing plants will not be defect free. The FDA considers defects to be maggots, thrips, insect fragments, "foreign matter," mold, rodent hairs, and insect and mammalian feces. What I found shocking was the levels of defects that could be present in our food. An ugly vegetable or a small strawberry, which are usually the best tasting, are not defects. It's actual contamination of our food that is allowed at what seems to be high levels.

Molds are also allowed in our food supply. Check out Title 21 from the Code of Federal Regulations for more information. The FDA does allow ingredients for food to have a percentage of mold and defects. This percentage is close to the highest—if not the highest—allowed in the world. There is even a process for reporting it. The problem is that all processed and ultra-processed food has been made with some form of mold in at least one ingredient but usually more. Most sugars, like dextrose, are liquid moldy corn sugars. The sugar is extracted from moldy corn and used to make your food ingredients. The regulations in place do not address the making of ingredients with mold. This can be a major issue for people with mold allergies and corn allergies. This is how some consumers became Conscientious Consumers (more on this group later).

Some companies spend more money to import lower mold value ingredients instead of buying from a company in the United States. This is a great example of how countries beyond the US could bring more transparency to their ingredients. The companies buying these higher quality ingredients also need to promote and disclose this fact so potential consumers can find them and buy from them. Many of the companies want to be seen as a healthier version of a food similar to those with the "organic" label.

The issues with processed and ultra-processed foods leads people to start looking seriously at organic foods. But what is organic and how does the consumer know what is truly organic and what is not? This all leads to the debate over what is an organic product. What I discovered is that organics in a grocery store are lower quality than organic bought directly from the farmer. Let's explore this category of foods more, since it tends to come up a lot in Hidden Consumer conversations.

ORGANIC LABELING

The health-based Hidden Consumer may start shopping for more food labeled "organic" to help them control their health issue(s). However, organic produce in grocery stores is coated with preservatives and sprays to help the product last longer on the shelf. It also helps kill any bugs that could be harmful to the other products in the store.

The USDA regulates what can be called "organic." There are multiple steps and regulations each farm needs to pass in order for it to follow USDA Organic standards. These standards are broken down into three groups: Produce and Grains; Meat, Dairy and Eggs; and Packaged Goods.

Here are the quick descriptions from the USDA website:

1. Produce and grains can only use natural fertilizers, use eco-friendly pest control, and protect soil and water.
2. Meat, dairy, and eggs must be from animals that freely roam the outdoors, producers that protect animal welfare, and with no growth hormones or antibiotics.
3. Packaged goods cannot use genetically modified organisms (GMOs), must be traceable from farm to store, and no artificial colors, flavors, or preservatives can be used.

The term "organic" is protected by law. This means no company should use this term, or specific variations listed by the USDA, without being certified through the USDA Organic Standards.

However, the next time you go the grocery store, check the items that say "organic" then look for the USDA seal. How many have it? You will find companies who make the claim without backing it up with certification. The bright side is they will be caught. The USDA does have auditors and inspectors in the field to stop false claims. One of the services I provide through Hidden Consumers Consulting is an assessment of your certifications. If you are making claims that are not verifiable, we will recommend you remove the false claim, or we will end our contract. Ethical marketing standards are important to us.

The USDA Organic symbol means this company has certified this product as organic. For example, in looking at a package of organic beef, the information is backed up by listing the certified ranch and location. In this case, it's the TMB Ranch in Virgina. TMB does not mean "text me back." In this example, the packaging states TMB Ranch is the source of the meat. This qualifies the seller as using a traceable source for their product and claims.

The same can be applied to the term "Fresh Whole Young Chickens." The company needs to prove the chickens were humanely raised, vegetarian fed, cage-free, given no antibiotics ever, given no added hormones, source verified, and traceable to a certified ranch.

These standards each have their own auditing process. If we look at the chicken example, these claims would need to be verified:

- **"Cage-free"** means the animal is not confined prior to the butchering process.
- The **"humanely raised"** claim is a gray area. There are no defined regulations or requirements on what animal welfare claims should be.
- **"Vegetarian feed"** means there are documented controls to ensure the animal ate a specific diet: a signed document of animal's diet to support the claim, and a written description of the product tracing.
- **"No antibiotics ever."** To use this claim, source animals cannot be administered antibiotics in their feed, water or by injections at any point in the production process. This includes ionophores which are recognized as antibiotics by the Food Safety and Inspection Service (FSIS).
- **"No added hormones."** For poultry this is an interesting claim to make since no hormones are approved for use or in production of poultry. Basically, this animal should be hormone free.
- **"Source verified and traceable to the [name of ranch]."** This is documentation that shows where the animal was born, where it was raised, and where it went for slaughter.

All of this is necessary to keep minimum guidelines in place for the industry to remain somewhat honest. We have all heard stories about the less-than-truthful companies. We've seen in the news how large companies are sued for violating marketing guidelines and regulations. The hope is when they do eventually get audited, such discrepancies are caught, and they remove the language. Most will probably pay the fine and move on with their day. In some cases, the fine is cheaper than being truthful with the public.

DISABILITIES

I want to start by saying **"disabled"** is not a bad word. It is not a negative. It is a descriptor that helps the world understand that some people (me included) need to achieve their end goal using a different set of procedures compared to able-bodied people. It is people with a closed, abelist mindset that make "disability" and "disabled" a negative.

This Hidden Consumer group is about more than just food. There are various ways this group of people are ignored or denied access. Much of what we do at Hidden Consumers Consulting is to bring **all** ideal clients to a brand's door. That includes those with disabilities. Whether you are online or have a brick-and-mortar location, you need to understand your ideal client can also have a disability. This is the fourth group of Hidden Consumers.

Those with various forms of disability from mobility to sensory to mental want to participate in the world around them. The problem is, we are often denied. Whether it be your website that is not accessible, or your brick-and-mortar location is unreachable, obstacles keep us from giving companies money.

I can go to any strip mall in Southern California and not have wheelchair access to 99 percent of the stores. Even if I can get through the front door, I have no maneuverability in the store. Sales floors are packed with shelves and products to such an extent that access is denied to those with mobility and sensory issues. There is a lot of griping in the small business community around physical locations being shut down due to lack of accessibility. The blame is put on the disabled person. How dare they demand access to a store!

The blame is bullshit. There are laws that require businesses to have space to allow wheelchair users safe access and mobility around a store. If you are going to have a brick-and-mortar location, you need to be accessible to all people. Why limit your potential earnings by only allowing a select percentage of the population to shop from you?

One of the biggest issues is how able-bodied business owners will claim disability access on their Google business profile just to increase business. But it backfires. As an active member and wheelchair user in the National Association of Women Business Owners (NAWBO), it is imperative to me that our events be accessible. When others picked locations in the past, they would look to see if the business said they were wheelchair friendly. The reality was these businesses often were not. I could not even get through the door without assistance. But this is normal. Many able-bodied people do not care about access to all. They have no concept of what it means to be denied access to events or locations because of mobility.

The enforcement of the law will vary based on where you live. Unless pressured to enforce the law, accessibility is not going to happen. It has become even more of a problem since the pandemic. One of the strip malls centers I shop at removed between 50 to 75 percent of their handicap parking spots. This creates issues for me because I need extra space to get out of my vehicle. Those lovely blue lines that tell you not to park in a specific area? They are so a disabled person can get out of a vehicle and not ding up your car door. By removing handicap parking spots, you deny me access through limiting a person's ability to get out of their car. I drove away instead of shopping there because I could not find a safe parking space for myself. Those businesses lose money every time a disabled person must drive away instead of shopping there. Physical access is not the only issue. Digital access is worse because standards are still being set.

If a brand's website is also inaccessible, it limits the company's sales potential. We use an accessible plugin / app when we help clients create websites, but the problem is even the applications are not 100-percent compliant. There is work I do on the backend to increase accessibility, but I still cannot get a full 100-percent compliance. It takes constant work to be accessible online. My biggest gripe is that accessibility should not be this hard for the micro or small business owner. Every business should have the ability to reach all their ideal clients regardless of technical ability.

This may seem off topic, but it is an integral part of the work I do to support Hidden Consumers with disabilities. When I work with clients to be transparent in their ingredients, I also look at how accessible they are to the wider world. An ADA section is in my assessment. I focus on tools around those who are colorblind, naming standards for links, sections descriptions, alt text on images, and so on. All of this ensures that as many of your ideal clients as possible can find you and see, or hear, your website clearly. Because at the end of the day, those who shop based on health issues and risks may also be disabled and need to know that your product is safe for them.

CONSCIENTIOUS CONSUMERS

The final Hidden Consumer group is the Conscientious Consumer. Everyone knows someone who fits this description. They want to protect animals and the environment. If you ask this group why they care about the environment so much, their response will probably be because they live here. They may also have health issues due to their former lifestyle and have chosen to be more conscientious about the food they eat. This is why I believe we are seeing an increase in people joining the vegan or vegetarian lifestyle or even switching to plant-based diets. This consumer will have various levels of knowledge on everything from corporate farming to soil and water pollution to GMOs.

The other key with Conscientious Consumers is they watch documentaries on our food and water and movies based on true stories. In documentaries like *King Corn* or movies like *Dark Waters*, they show this consumer group, as well as other thoughts around the food, chemicals, and other industries that affect the day-to-day life of everyday people. Every conversation I have with a Conscientious Consumer ends up with them asking if I read this book, or watched that documentary or movie. They want to know my opinion based on my personal experiences and the impact it had on my life. One of these life impacting experiences was having to understand the importance of corporate farming and how it negatively affected my health. Let's dig into this issue and others that affect the Conscientious Consumer.

Corporate Farming and Its Impact

The number of subsidies in farming combined with family farmers having a hard time finding successors for farms led to the corporate farming industry. The "pro" of corporate farming is the lower cost of food. But what is the cost to the consumer in terms of health? The lower cost is attributed to creating the ingredients needed to make our processed and ultra-processed foods, as well as lower cost meats. Overall, food science is having a negative impact on human life. This type of farming has also led to poor animal husbandry practices, environmental damage, and illness, including cancer, for the people who live around the corporate farms.

Animal Welfare

For the Consciousness Consumer, learning about animal cruelty goes even further when learning about the lifespan of the different animals raised on corporate farms.

FarmUSA.org is a group focused on the Farm Animal Rights Movement. They focus on the vegetarian movement as well as animal rights advocacy. The reason they do what they do is because of how animals are raised, and killed, due to the animal's ability to make money for a business.

The group shares some graphic information about animal cruelty related to corporate farming. For example, they discuss how male chicks are ground up alive or suffocated because they don't lay eggs.

Female pigs live in a constant state of pregnancy and have their piglets torn away shortly after birth. The piglets have a lifespan of roughly six months. They are fattened up and slaughtered for human consumption. Dairy cows suffer a similar fate in order to constantly supply milk. FarmUSA's website further discusses the horrible conditions for pigs, dairy cattle, and even fish and other aquatic animals.

Everyone has seen the images and video of animals shoved into small pens and stepping on each other. These types of farming practices have led to an increase of bird flu amongst chickens that skyrocketed prices at the end of 2023. It is also why bird flu is now being seen in cattle and humans. The other factor is the low-quality diet barn animals are fed. The irony is that these practices are also why chickens and other animals are on antibiotics.

Animal health on larger farms is constantly threatened by the living conditions they endure. Just like humans, the antibiotics eventually don't protect the animal. There are studies that also point to antibiotic resistance in humans because of the animals using the same antibiotics used by people. In 2024, Tyson said they were going to stop using antibiotics meant for humans in their chickens. But they did not detail what exact medications will be given and what they consider to be human antibiotics. Like most food companies, they expect the populations to take them at their word and not show or detail what they actually intend to do.

In the Midwest and other corn-growing regions, it is common knowledge that hogs, chickens, and cows eat corn not designed for human consumption. According to the Iowa Corn Growers Association, only 9 percent of corn grown in the US is grown for residential use, while 91 percent of corn is grown for animal consumption or products. I have seen this percentage as high as 99 percent for animals and 1 percent for humans. Field corn is not only used for animal feed. It is also used to make ethanol fuel, alcohol, toothpaste, medications, crayons, paper, glue, tires, vitamins, fireworks, carpet, and degradable plastics.

GMO corn feeds the animals that supply the meat in the grocery stores. The question that presents itself is, can animals digest corn? Michigan State University Extension investigated this common discussion to determine if it was truth or fallacy. Here's their bottom line on the argument: The presence of whole corn kernels leads them to the conclusion that no, animals cannot completely digest it, and costs are not justified.

Corn is somewhat digestible by the animals, but is it converted to energy or is it stored for fat? If you look at pasture-raised cattle versus grain-fed cattle, you see an extreme difference in the meat. Grain-fed cattle and hogs are fattier. There is marbling in the meat, and some say it has more flavor, while pasture-raised cattle are leaner and have less marbling to their meat. The other difference between the two is grass-fed beef is lower in calories and fat with higher levels of Omega-3 fatty acids. Personally, I find the grass-fed to have better taste. Based on my own experience of having to drastically change my diet, I think processed and ultra-processed foods destroy our taste buds.

Think about people who have traveled to Europe. People who typically eat less-processed foods find Europe to have amazing quality food with a depth of flavor they cannot find in the United States. However, the people who live primarily on processed foods find European food too disgusting and they come back complaining about how terrible the food is. I don't believe this is a coincidence. My friends who live overseas and have visited the United States generally did not enjoy a majority of their eating experiences here either. So why is there a difference in flavor between grass-fed and grain-fed? It all comes down to how the animals store their food.

Grain-fed or corn-fed animals store food as fat. Most of the meat on the market is mostly fat due to the amount of corn feed the animal consumes and lack of movement for corporate farmed animals. All that marbling people rave about? It's animal fat. Let's be honest, that's what makes bacon a hot commodity. But for Hidden Consumers who need to eat healthier or even protect animal rights, the amount of fat is a testament to the poor treatment of the animal.

The other issue is that corn in steers' diets leads to higher levels of illness. Yes, it can digest corn, but corn is not necessarily healthy for the steer to eat. Corn can lead to extremely painful illnesses in cattle. According to the Beef Council in 2022, one of the illnesses of concern was acidosis. This is a digestive disorder when too much acid is created, and the animal cannot neutralize it.

But why is corn so prevalent in animal feed if it makes our food sick? One, corn is cheap, not just inexpensive. Two, grass-fed-only animals have a lower efficiency ratio of feed to meat. Cows in particular need more crops than the meat you can get from them. On the other hand, chickens have a higher ratio. You can get a pound of chicken with fewer crops.

This means corporate or factory farms are going to feed their animals, cows and hogs in particular, the cheapest food source possible. However, the farmers are making less money today on hogs than in 1982. They are making $2 less per pound to be precise. On top of that, Iowa has lost 90 percent of its family-scale hog farms as factory farms rapidly expand. The more money lost in one industry over time, and the cheaper the feed available, the more likely corn is to be fed at factory farms.[5]

I learned about the poor diet of hogs and pigs through making a mistake.

We found a safe farmer in Zumbrota, Minnesota. We found him at the St. Paul Farmers Market. It was the middle of winter in Minnesota, and I was tired of steak and potatoes for every meal. He had a package of St. Louis ribs in my safe packaging, and I bought them. They were the best ribs I had ever eaten. However, the three-day migraine was not worth it. The next Sunday, I asked him about the ribs. From that conversation, I researched more into animal feed versus food for humans. As a super sensitive Hidden Consumer, it made sense that I reacted the way I did.

Today, usable farmland is constantly used to grow non-human consumable corn, which is feeding our food and making us sick. The numbers from Iowa are staggering when you consider how many animals they need to feed each day. In Iowa, there are 80 million farm animals compared to three million people.

The other issue is the amount of environmental pollution the 80 million animals are creating every day. Barns produce a massive amount of feces that in turn, due to the low-quality diet the animals are on, lead to soil and water pollution along with other issues. Animal living conditions combined with diet are having an impact on our environment.

Environmental

The environment is a growing concern for many consumers, from climate change to soil pollution, to water contamination. People want to know that the company they buy from shares those concerns and is committed to improving, or at least not negatively impacting, the planet. To understand why a Conscientious Consumer is concerned, a company can better refine their marketing to attract and retain new customers. However, the Federal Trade Commission also has standards on how companies can discuss environmental claims. I don't believe most marketing firms understand the legal liability of the work they do around what they say a company does versus the reality of the situation. Let's explore some of these environmental issues.

Soil Pollution

In 2021, the UN reported an increase in organic contaminants in soils. When most people think of corporate farming or factory farms, they think of Iowa. The people of Iowa have struggled with corporate farming on a scale that is impacting not only how the animals are treated, but also the environment.

Here is how the report defined organic fertilizers:

"Organic fertilizers commonly used in agriculture include animal manure, compost, septic sludge, sewage sludge, municipal biosolids and food processing wastes (Khan et al., 2018). The beneficial aspect of the use of organic fertilizer is the improvement in soil health through organic carbon enrichment and slow release of nutrients. However, it may also become a source of soil pollution due to the mineralization of organic nitrogen, increasing the nitrate concentration, and the presence of trace elements, per fluorinated alkylated substances (PFASs), brominated flame retardants and other toxic substances (Gottschall et al., 2017; Petersen et al., 2003)."[6]

The other factor the report mentions is that antibiotics are also primarily composed of corn-derivatives:

"Antimicrobials are routinely provided to animals prophylactically to prevent disease but also to promote growth. It is reported that 75 to 90 percent of the administered antimicrobials are not completely metabolized in human and animal bodies (Marshall and Levy, 2011), are excreted and accumulate in animal manure, municipal wastewater, wastewater sludge and biosolids (Bouki, Venieri and Diamadopoulos, 2013; Daghrir and Drogui, 2013; Wu et al., 2013)."

Not only are we dealing with a higher rate of antimicrobial-resistance, but we could also see an increase in sensitivity.

The other issue is plastics being used for mulching in the fields. Current trends are for using biodegradable plastic, which is more than likely made from corn. On top of that, we have soil organisms that rely on soil particles for their nutrients. According to the UN, "A significant risk associated with the presence of plastics in soil is due to the presence of micro- and nano-plastics, which can be ingested by organisms that feed on soil particles and transfer them to the food chain (Huerta-Lwanga et al., 2017)."[7]

The Corn Refiners of America proudly boast about components in a variety of animal feed types. In poultry feed corn, gluten meal provides energy, essential fatty and amino acids, and helps give egg yolks their golden yellow color. In pig feed, corn germ meal is rich in highly digestible amino acids and is a good source of protein for pig diets.[8]

If you look up how most of these feeds are "enhanced" you will see it all goes back to not only corn but also corn derivatives. Next, their waste is used to "enrich" the crops soil. Now you have a buildup of corn-based chemicals and pharmaceuticals, from antibiotics and other medicines given to the animals, in our soil.

Prior to my birth, and for about two years after, my dad was a traveling farmhand. He, my mom, and eventually me, would move from farm to farm in the upper Midwest. We lived in a camper near the fields. This may be a key to why I seem to be super sensitive to corn and corn derivatives.

One of the many health issues I have is my lymphatic system never fully formed in utero. We know for sure that 50 percent of my lymph nodes do not exist in my right arm in comparison to my left arm. It is possible that with the proximity my parents lived to fields means the pesticides used may be a factor in my lymphatic system and other health concerns. The overall effect of pesticides is long-term. You don't just stop using it and it magically disappears from the soil or body. Dichlorodiphenyltrichloroethane (DDT) is an example of this.

In 1972, the FDA banned the use of DDT in fields for its harmful effects on the human body, including altering our DNA. The Center for Disease Control (CDC) defines DDT as: "Dichlorodiphenyltrichloroethane (DDT) is an insecticide used in agriculture. The United States banned the use of DDT in 1972. Some countries outside the United States still use DDT to control mosquitoes that spread malaria." This is from the Centers for Disease Control and Prevention.

The CDC offers a fact sheet on DDT. It covers how people were exposed, the health effects, and current levels as late as 2002. According to the fact sheet from the Centers for Disease Control and Prevention, "DDT and its related chemicals persist for a long time in the environment and in animal tissues."

This is one example of many that may be part of the problem with current increases in allergies and cancers across the United States. As I was going through the learning process of my sensitivity I started to wonder if issues like DDT were part of the problem as friends were sharing their home garden produce. In the long run knowing won't help me; but if there is a connection, can we save future generations from having allergies like we do?

I realized on my journey that soil was a problem for me. The whole emphasis of saving the environment in elementary school? Not so much in reality. From poor farming practices to not understanding the biomes within our soil, we are creating an environment for more allergies to develop while depleting our soil. The WHO has been looking into fertilizers and how different chemicals affect the land.

One common chemical used in fertilizers, 2,4-Dichlorophenoxyacetic acid, is used on multiple fields. This chemical not only kills the soil biome, but it has health risks for humans. What is a soil biome? It is the organisms that live in the soil that help reduce pollution and maintain a healthy soil. A healthy soil benefits the plants and those that eat them. Key nutrients that we need from plants come from a healthy soil biome. I love gardening and turning my entire yard into a large native plant garden. I don't like bugs. But I know spiders and roly-polies are part of what the garden needs to maintain a healthy balanced soil structure.

What I find interesting is you can go for years without using synthetic fertilizers and pesticides and still have a reaction. The current research is showing chemical-based fertilizers kill the soil biome. In turn, this depletes the soil of healthy organisms forcing the farmer or grower to continue to use the chemical-based fertilizer. To overcome this obstacle, the farmer needs to replace the soil biome.

One company doing this work, Biome Makers, is showing how to bring back the soil biome after fertilizers and other chemicals have killed it. I first heard about them while listening to the *Wine for Normal People Podcast*. The host interviewed one of the founders to discuss farming practices and the impact it has on soil and crop production. I was not able to reach anyone for comment, but I did get to attend a few of their webinars.

Biome Makers looks at common challenges for farmers and soil pollution. Their goal is to help solve these challenges while studying and rebuilding the soil biome. They understand that soil is a symbiotic ecosystem. If it is effectively managed, you can increase yield and quality of crops. This occurs through understanding the biodiversity within the soil, how it functions, and how it creates overall soil health.

Understanding the effects of soil pollution on the foods we eat is an important skill for any Hidden Consumer. I had an amazing group of people around me when I started my journey. It was through eating vegetables grown in friends' gardens that led me to do more research. I had to start asking qualifying questions before I could take their garden produce. Did you plant this corn in previous years? Hard pass if the answer was yes. Did you use store-bought fertilizers in your garden? Another hard no if so. I eventually learned that cow manure as a fertilizer was an issue for me because of the amount of corn in their diets.

My paternal grandfather was a farmer. I remember listening to his conversations about rotating the crops and what fields needed to rest at the end of the season. I remember hearing his discussions on where to let the cows graze and in what fields. He would give his land time to rest, and the cows would add natural fertilizer, the kind without corn or antibiotics. His milk cattle were raised on a diet of hay. During the rest period, he would pasture his milking cows to eat the weeds and grass while depositing natural fertilizer in the fields. These practices are crucial to the environment and soil biomes while also impacting our food supply. The research has also connected synthetic fertilizers to human illness for decades.

The practice of pasturing cows in resting fields means the farmer is replenishing the soil biome, just like my grandfather did. When plants are grown in a field, they absorb the field and soil nutrients which translates to nutrients for the humans who eat the food after the harvest. The rest is needed to replenish those nutrients to continue to grow viable crops for generations to come. When you don't allow this process to happen, you kill the soil biome, in turn eliminating the nutrients. In some cases, like in the wine industry, soil nutrients can vary from field to field. This is why true wine varies in taste based on the land it is grown on.

The flip side to this issue is by killing the soil biome you are always killing nature's ability to control pests that destroy crops. The use of pesticides only works until the next generation of pests improves their ability to adapt to the pesticide.

I may be biased, but our country's need to kill the family farm and replace it with corporate farming is part of the issue here. Family farmers are more likely to practice organic, or even biodynamic farming to grow food. Corporate farms are more likely to be the environmental polluters.

Another way corporate farming contributes to soil pollution is the issue of fertilizer. The number of livestock being kept on corporate farms means the amount of fertilizer made is more than the fields can handle. They are dealing with runoff that is polluting wells, streams, rivers, and lakes according to the EPA.[9]

Biosolids are also used as fertilizers. They are organic matter recycled from sewage, which is used as fertilizers to increase soil nutrient content, and are also a problem for soil pollution. The United Nations estimates that 95 percent of microplastics that go through wastewater treatment plants can be classified as biosolids, which means they are also a source of soil pollution.[10]

Leftover plastic debris is becoming a global concern. These plastics are not fully decomposed and are found in our fields, and in water.[11] The issue is that the microplastics are not only changing the composition of the soil and killing off micro-organisms that clean the soil—they are also being found in animal and human stomachs. The overall effect is they are changing the soil composition with fewer nutrients, stunting plant growth and yield.

Think about that plastic water bottle you use that is made from GMO corn. Corn-based plastics do not fully break down. These pollutants are in everything from pesticides to mineral and organic fertilizers (manure and sewage sludge) to irrigation wastewater to packaging to rural wastes. The microplastics being found in human stomachs, as well as our soil and water are in part from corn.[12]

My favorite example is boxed wine. My corn allergy helped me become a wine snob. If I could be a sommelier, I would. Too many wines are aged in stainless steel that uses citric acid and other corn derivatives in the fermentation and aging process, and I cannot tolerate it. Now in the case of boxed wine, it is usually a blend of varietals, fermented and aged in stainless steel then put in food-grade plastic bags to sell to the consumer. The boxed wine you drink also deposits nano plastics in your stomach.

Recently, microplastics have been discovered in human stomachs. This could be one of the causes of microplastics in our environments. The connection lies between pollution, current farming practices focused on corn, and animals raised only on corn.

Let's take Iowa Corporate Farms as our example. They grow corn mostly for animal consumption, not human consumption. The cows, pigs, and chickens eat the corn. This corn has been planted in soil that has been stripped of nutrients. These 80 million animals create manure every day. Now you have an overabundance of manure that is not healthy for the land. When used on the crops, it doesn't add nutritional value, and the amount produced is polluting the environment.

There are people in the Conscientious Consumer group who understand this connection between farming practices and the effects on the human body. There are even watchdog groups in Washington, D.C. fighting to keep our soil safe from the additional use of plastics as mulch for crops. Believe it or not, 92 percent of plastics are not recyclable. This also means they do not easily decompose in the soil.

Pesticides / Chemicals / Pharmaceuticals and Our Water

A concern for many Conscientious Consumers is climate change and water protection. There is a link between how animals are raised on corporate farms and the negative impact these farms have on the environment.

A growing number of organic contaminants are classified as emerging concerns in soil pollution research, and much less is understood about fate and behavior. According to the UN, the rapid expansion in products used, particularly pharmaceutical, personal care products, and pesticides, has outstripped the ability of the scientific community to fully research the threats posed, both singly and in combination with other compounds, to allow comprehensive risk assessment and regulation.[13]

Biosolids, pharmaceuticals, pesticides, and everything from hygiene products to cosmetics and skin care are all adding to our pollution levels. Even medications are a problem. It's part of the reason some cities have drop areas or specific days for unused medication. The other reason is to keep the community safe. What the United Nations found was that these substances had been released into the environment through wastewater and wastewater sludge. Some of these substances can also disrupt hormonal systems of living organisms, which can cause adverse health effects. They are known as endocrine disruptors.[14]

Pesticides, chemicals, and pharmaceuticals have all been shown to kill our soil biomes. The more we use, the more dependent we become on the product. Thus, we continue to harm and destroy the environment and out water around us. The stripped healthy biome leads to fewer nutrient rich crops which, in turn, hurts people.

GMOs

I have yet to have a discussion on food intolerances and allergies where the topic of GMOs does not come up. It is automatically assumed my allergy stems from GMO crops. I don't believe this, but I do believe GMO farming is part of a larger environmental issue we are facing today. The Conscientious Consumer will have their own thoughts around GMOs.

I know a lot of people who avoid eating GMOs because they fear science. Food that is genetically modified may sound bad for people. However, the reality is many of our foods have been genetically modified over time. Many of the fruits and vegetables we know today are not the same from years gone by. I do question two aspects of today's GMOs. One, what is the process of genetically modifying today? If it is in a lab environment with corn derivatives, I am obviously going to personally have a problem. Two, what is the environmental impact on the soil biome of growing GMOs? Yep, GMOs pollute our environment. For the farmers there is an additional issue of higher rates of crop failure. In Monsanto vs US Farmers, the following was noted:

"Not only do farmers suffer from Monsanto's legal warfare, but many also experience crop failure due to deficiencies in Monsanto's

genetically engineered seed. A number of these farmers have taken their
own legal action against the company in attempts to recoup substantial
financial loss." [15]

Monsanto has strict guidelines for farmers who choose to or are coerced into using only their product. The information is based on what research I could find, which is limited due to Monsanto's tight control of all things GMO related. Most of the research is biased due to being funded by the biotech industry, which profits from GMOs.

The harm Monsanto and GMOs have done to the environment is coupled with how farmers manage their land and how they farm. First, according to the Center for Food Safety, farmers are not allowed to save their seeds for later use. As part of Monsanto's technology agreement with farmers, which has a 31-page supplementary publication, the farmer waives rights to their private property and personal records as well. Some of these waivers allow access to their private property, personal records, and access to activities held by third parties. These refers mostly to the USDA Farm Service Crop reporting information on any land farmed by the grower. This agreement removes the farmers' right to manage their land as they see fit in regard to the exact methods used to deal with insects in order to ensure crop yields. The problem is that the seed itself is deficient.

An example of this deficiency is the cotton industry. The GMO cotton plant continually fails to protect against bollworms and budworms. This leaves the farmer having to spend extra time and money to protect the crops. On top of low germination rates, lower yields, and smaller bolls, this leads to difficulty in harvesting the crop.

The real reason to avoid GMOs is the impact they have on our environment. At the end of the day, a GMO product is only about creating more yield, thus increasing corporate profits. The question is: Does it live up to the hype? Do GMOs increase yields? Do they provide nutritional value?

According to Food & Water Watch, an environmental nonprofit, no. "Studies on certain GMO crops have found little to no yield improvements, and long-term studies of organic farming show that organic can match conventional agriculture's yields."[16] From a nutritional standpoint, it seems to have no benefit. If you take the case of "golden rice" and the claim it was to help emerging countries cure vitamin A deficiency, it did not. The nutritional value of a GMO product is nil. The use of fertilizers and pesticides destroys the soil biome where the vegetable or fruit gets its nutrients.

So how do GMOs impact our environment? GMO crops are engineered to resist chemicals like weed killers. When a farmer uses GMO crops, they need to use fertilizers engineered for GMOs and pesticides and other chemicals throughout the growing season. Both the manufactured fertilizers and pesticides, plus other chemicals used, destroy the soil. These are part of our soil pollution problem. Additionally, as nature adapts to the pesticides and chemicals, either more needs to be applied or a strong version needs to be created. This leads to more environmental damage.

The other less-talked-about issue with GMOs is how they spread. According to the Center for Food Safety, "In some parts of this country and Canada, conventional and organic farmers alike have lost premium markets as they have been forced to sell contaminated crops into the genetically engineered crop stream. Crop contamination is a serious problem that, so far, Monsanto has only been using to its advantage."[17]

Like all crops, they produce pollen that spreads on the wind. Farmers who don't want GMOs often find the crops growing in their field. The seeds blow in from miles away. If the farmer is an organic farmer, this can lead to problems on multiple levels. Take into consideration that organic farmers are not allowed to use GMOs. The time and effort they put into being an organic farm goes out the window if they cannot stop the encroachment of a crop they do not want in their fields.

Another obstacle is transparency. Monsanto and the biotech industry are fighting hard to have the term "GMO" removed from product labels. I, personally, don't want to buy a product that is destroying our environment. Consumers need to be allowed to make that decision for themselves. Part of this comes into play when attempting to export GMO crops to Europe. The Center for Food Safety also reports that, "The American Farm Bureau estimates that farmers have lost $300 million per year due to European markets refusing to take genetically engineered corn from the US Trade officials at the US State Department believe the US could lose as much as $4 billion annually in agricultural exports to the European Union due to the recent enactment of labeling and traceability requirements by the EU."

This is a great example of how the EU is doing more to protect people than we do in the United States. The Hidden Consumer solution is that it can be used anywhere in the world. The goal is creating a transparency around ingredients and materials that exceeds all government regulations. But products around the world still have marketing problems that leave the consumer distrustful and not willing to take a buying risk.

2

Marketing Problems Today

TODAY THE BIGGEST ISSUES for Hidden Consumers relate to false marketing claims and lack of consumer education. People with medical concerns, like allergies or intolerances, may depend on labeling like "dairy-free" or "sugar-free" to maintain their health. However, these terms are not always used accurately. Unfortunately, all many marketers see are phrases they can use to make a quick buck. Companies do not seem to be concerned with the potential risk to those who buy the product based on the marketing claim. The consumer may know how to look for specific ingredients but won't know all the ways dairy or sugar is being used in a product they are considering purchasing.

Some of the key problems in food industry marketing are greenwashing, misuse of seals and certifications, misuse of product terms, how to engage a millennial consumer, and bioengineered products.

GREENWASHING

The number one issue in today's marketing is false environmental claims, also known as greenwashing. According to the United Nations, greenwashing claims lead the consumer to believe a company is doing more to help the environment then they really are and promoting false solutions to the environmental crisis. These tactics lead to an obstacle in tackling climate change.

This type of marketing applies to all industries that have an impact on the environment. Companies who put profit over the planet or ethics are slowly being held accountable for false claims. This is no different in the food and beverage industry.

There have been five major class-action lawsuits against companies for greenwashing in the last few years. The top five companies involved were Keurig K-Cup, Teracycle, Oatly, Starbucks, and Innocent. The article "5 Food and Drink Brands Called Out for Greenwashing and the Lessons We Can Learn" summarizes each lawsuit. Here is a quick synopsis of the article and each company's issue:

1. Keurig K-Cup paid out $10 million to consumers for claiming their packaging was fully recycleable while not being fully open about how materials recovery facilities processed used cups.

2. TerraCycle faced a lawsuit from an environmental group with claims of forcing consumers to pay recycling costs. Major brands like Gerber, Coca-Cola, and Late July Snacks had the TerraCycle logo on certain products. This led consumers to believe that packaging, when it reached its end, could be recycled for free. However, TerraCycle's partnerships were limited, and free recycling was with "limited availability."

3. Oatly had its high-profile campaign banned by the UK's Advertising Standards Authority for overstating the carbon footprint difference between oat milk and dairy milk. Oatly had made a blanket statement that all of their products had a better carbon footprint than all dairy milk. The truth was only one of Oatly's products could make that claim. On top of that, Oatly

referred to only **one** climate expert for their claim instead of a larger group of scientists.

4. Starbucks' rolled out what they called a "more sustainable" straw-less lid with the claim they were reducing their environmental footprint. The truth was that the one plastic lid contained more plastic than the original lid and straw combined. On top of that, the world experts also pointed out that only 9 percent of the world's plastic is actually recyclable.

5. Innocent, a smoothie brand, overstated their environment claims and had their advertisements banned by the UK's Advertising Standards Authority. Consumer groups complained to ASA stating that Innocent's environmental claims exaggerated the benefits of recycling versus throwing in a landfill. Consumers could interpret the ad to mean buying Innocent's products would be a positive benefit on the environment, when in reality it was not.[18]

These are the not the first cases and they are absolutely not the last. Cases are being battled every day over misleading claims and overstatements. Other companies we could talk about are Volkswagen, Toyota, Kohl's, Walmart, and Goldman Sachs to name a few. And this list doesn't include those who have only been accused.

The author said succinctly, consumers are savvier than before. In the case of the Hidden Consumer, they have to be savvy.

Is there any way we can send a kudos or an award to the ASA for staying on top of false marketing claims? In the United States we do have guidelines from the Federal Trade Commission called "FTC's Green Guides" to tackle greenwashing in multiple industries. The "Federal Register" is a 12-page guide for the Use of Environmental Marketing Claims. I am not about to go page by page, because it is a typical government document. Here's the short version: Don't overstate your environmental impact.

It sounds simple, right? Be honest and differentiate between product, packaging, and service. Yet, according to the FTC website, at least 20 cases have been filed in the last nine years. Major brands have fallen to poor marketing choices and overstating their actual benefits.

Let's use bamboo as an example. The FTC has an article "How to Avoid Bamboozling Your Customers" to discuss the proper ways of marketing a bamboo-like product. Consumers know the benefits of bamboo. It's environmentally friendly, it grows quickly and doesn't need pesticides. Awesome! But in marketing, that's not the whole story.

Almost all, if not all, of the bamboo-labeled products on the market are actually made from rayon. Which is probably made from corn. When a company doesn't use real bamboo, all the positive environmental factors go away. But companies will greenwash the product and say its bamboo. This is why the FTC says you have to label fake bamboo products with the label "mechanically processed bamboo."

If you are using authentic bamboo, you need to be able to back up the claim. You will need to provide scientific tests and analyses to show the actual bamboo fiber. As a brand, you should not trust the claims of your supplier without first verifying them. You will be held accountable if the claims turn out to be false.[19]

Beyond bamboo, the FTC has regulations and guides for almost every industry from light fixtures to trash to seals and certifications. Make sure your marketing team knows how to look up regulations in your industry to keep you out of court.

MISUSE OF THIRD-PARTY CERTIFICATIONS

Certifications can be helpful to the Hidden Consumer when the company is legitimately using proper certifications. Companies falsifying third-party certifications has become such an issue that in 2012 the FTC revised their Green Guides to include a section on "Seals and Certifications."

In my early days of dealing with food issues, "gluten-free" (GF) was just hitting the market. Everyone was claiming they had a GF product. Those with true gluten issues were disappointed to still not be able to find pre-packaged products that were safe. Certifications helped bring clarity and traceable processes to back up claims, such as "gluten-free." The problem is, there are still marketing teams that use terms as a marketing ploy rather than knowing if a product qualifies to use a specific term. They also clearly don't have the certification to back up their claims.

Today, some Hidden Consumers depend on seeing a "certified by..." seal to give them confidence in their purchase. However, for the vast majority of Hidden Consumers, the seal is a starting point. Not everything that has a third-party seal or certification will fit each consumer's requirements. Let's use the Plant Based Food Association as an example.

The Plant Based Food Association offers third-party certification for plant-based products. This is different from Whole Food Plant Based Certification through WFPB.org. The distinction is important. People who look only for the "plant based" moniker will be OK eating some of the ingredients used in plant-based products. But for the Hidden Consumer focused on Whole Food Plant Based, the basic plant-based certification includes ingredients they don't want to consume.

My strategic branding partner and her husband changed their lifestyle to Whole Food Plant Based in 2020. For them, when going over the list of companies that were certified as plant-based, they did not find anything they could eat. The problem was too many lab-created ingredients were still included in the ingredients list. For example, Beyond Meat is a member and makes a food they will not buy because of the ingredients.

Whole Food Plant Based Certification claims to have stricter requirements around their process and ingredients that can be used in products. I did not find any companies with the seal. WFPB.org does not list the companies that carry the certification.

Even though the FTC regulates third-party seals and certifications, it does not mean the certified item is safe. Each Hidden Consumer needs to do their own research to determine if a specific seal or certification fits their needs.

MISUSE OF PRODUCT TERMS

Product terms are not third-party certifications. These are the terms used by marketers to get you to buy their products. These are terms like "sugar-free" or "gluten-free" that are used even if the company does not have a seal showing they are certified to make those claims.

We all know the food and beverage industry uses marketing terms on their packaging to increase sales. There is a high percentage of these companies who do not even know if their products truly fit the term they are using to sell their product. This is why the Hidden Consumer has to have a greater depth of knowledge. They know they cannot always trust the industries to market truthfully.

The other issue with these claims is the regulations being skirted by companies who use them improperly. "Organic" is a highly regulated term by the USDA. Yet, you have probably seen products on the store shelves with this term and no USDA seal. Here are a few of the most popular, misunderstood, and misused terms currently in the industry.

Allergy-Free / Allergy-Friendly

Companies claiming to be allergy friendly are focused on sales and **only** the recognized allergens. They don't believe their product could kill someone. Enjoy Life is one brand many with unrecognized allergies could not tolerate. Enjoy Life was so focused on the FDA-recognized allergens that when sesame became a recognized allergen, it shut down almost all their production. They discontinued their products instead of using alternatives to sesame.

No company can say they are allergen-free. Someone will be allergic to what you sell. When companies tout being allergen free what they are saying is they don't understand allergies or how food and products are made.

A company's lack of knowledge in this field while trying to sell to the allergen community can be a deadly combination. Not everyone with an unrecognized allergen or intolerance knows what to look for. They expect the maker of a product to know what ingredients were used. I have seen too many people in my allergen communities get sick and end up hospitalized due to trusting a company's response to an ingredient question. As consumers, we cannot trust companies to know what is best for us. We must do research to keep ourselves safe.

This issue is not limited to brands in the grocery store. It happens at farmer's markets as well. The one I go to has a homemade fudge booth. It looks lovely, but I can guarantee you that 75 percent of their ingredients are derived from corn. Every single time I stop at their booth, they tell me, "Oh no that's not possible. Our fudge is safe." (Insert major eyeroll here). No, your product is not safe just because you say so. The Hidden Consumer needs to see your full ingredient list in order to feel confident and safe.

This information is not intended to turn companies away from how they make food for mass production. The intent is to help companies and consumers alike understand what the Hidden Consumer needs to consider before they purchase a product. When food companies are better educated on food then their customer service teams will be better educated, which leads to your brand having higher loyalty. Do you want to be a brand consumers can trust? Or a brand that everyone in the allergen community avoids and tells everyone who will listen to avoid?

Lactose / Dairy

In recent years, marketing departments and companies have confused the difference between "Lactose-Free" and Dairy-Free." As consumers, we have an idea of what it should mean, however, there is no set regulatory framework for defining each term. The biggest problem is that dairy is considered a major food allergen, which means these definitions are key to keeping people safe.

- **Lactose-free** products can be made from real dairy milk, but there are no FDA regulations or guidelines around the term. In 2018/2019 they did a sample collection and analysis of domestically manufactured, lactose-free dark chocolate products to check for milk allergens. In the research they state: "Milk is the most common undeclared food allergen, responsible for more than a third of all food product recalls caused by undeclared allergens in the US in the past decade.[2,3] Milk also has been observed to be the leading cause of consumer adverse reactions to foods recalled because of undeclared allergens,[4] and these foods included dark chocolate products."[20]
- **Dairy-free** products are made from plant sources such as nuts and grains. There are no regulatory standards around this terminology. In February 2023, the FDA did release a draft that was developed for the labeling of plant-based milk alternatives and voluntary nutrient statements. It "recommends that a plant-based milk alternative product that includes the term "milk" in its name (e.g., "soy milk" or "almond milk"), and that has a nutrient composition that is different than milk, include a voluntary

nutrient statement that conveys how the product compares with milk based on the US Department of Agriculture's (USDA) Food and Nutrition Service fluid milk substitutes nutrient criteria. For example, the label could say, "Contains lower amounts of Vitamin D and calcium than milk."[21]

■ **Non-dairy** falls under the dairy-free category, but once again, there is little to no actual guidance on how the term should be used or defined.

What this means for the consumer is that any company can use any term they want without understanding how the consumer is using it. I know people who are lactose and dairy intolerant and allergic. Over the last two years, many of these people have ended up in the ER due to reactions to undisclosed dairy in a product. One friend discovered a company hiding dairy by giving it a different name. This friend now knows how to look for other names for their allergen.

Gluten-Free

Gluten is the only allergen for which the FDA has a labeling rule for "absence of" claims.[22] The regulation defines "gluten-free" as meaning that the food either is inherently gluten-free or does not contain an ingredient that is:

1. a gluten-containing grain (e.g., spelt wheat);
2. derived from a gluten-containing grain that has not been processed to remove gluten (e.g., wheat flour);
3. derived from a gluten-containing grain that has been processed to remove gluten (e.g., wheat starch), if the use of that ingredient results in the presence of 20 parts per million (ppm) or more gluten in the food.

Also, any unavoidable presence of gluten in the food must be less than 20 ppm. The FDA did adjust their guidelines to meet Canada's 20 ppm rule. The other interesting fact on the Q & A sheet is they do not recommend people with celiac disease eat foods labeled "gluten-free."

Should consumers with celiac disease only be searching for foods labeled as "gluten-free" to consume safely in their diets? Not necessarily. Consumers with celiac disease should read and scrutinize labels to avoid gluten ingredients. "Gluten-free" is a voluntary claim that manufacturers can use in food labeling, provided that those foods meet all requirements for a "gluten-free" food. Some manufacturers may specially process or reformulate foods to be free of gluten and to be eligible to bear a "gluten-free" labeling claim.

Organic

I have already discussed organic foods in relation to their importance to the Hidden Consumer's overall health, but let's talk more in depth about it in terms of labeling standards. When it comes to "organic" the USDA (farm product) regulates it. Here is the definition from the USDA document Organic 101: What the USDA Organic Label Means:

> *"USDA certified organic foods are grown and processed according to federal guidelines addressing, among many factors, soil quality, animal raising practices, pest and weed control, and use of additives. Organic producers rely on natural substances and physical, mechanical, or biologically based farming methods to the fullest extent possible."*

Certified Organic products have gone through a long process of verification to prove they can make specific claims around the term "organic" and similar claims. The industry today has products on the market with USDA certification. This means if a product is claiming to be "organic" but has no USDA label, it is an unsubstantiated claim. This is also illegal. There are many Hidden Consumers who look for certain certifications, including the USDA certification, to verify they are closer to getting a safer product. Let's take a look at the primary categories of organic foods and how they are labeled:

Produce

According to the USDA, produce can be called organic if it's "certified to have grown on soil that had no prohibited substances applied for three years prior to harvest. Prohibited substances include most synthetic fertilizers and pesticides. In instances when a grower has to use a synthetic substance to achieve a specific purpose, the substance must first be approved according to criteria that examine its effects on human health and the environment."[23]

Organic foods are foods grown without the use of synthetic chemicals, like pesticides and fertilizers. This also used to mean they were not sprayed with synthetics after the food was harvested. The preservation of the food after the harvest is where it becomes a gray area for some of us with allergies. In my case, I look for farmers I can work with to buy my food. I can ask them what organic means to them and their processes.

I know based on my hypersensitivity level that organic foods from a grocery store are sprayed with preservatives so they keep longer in the stores and don't cause disease. But preservatives cannot be washed off. I'm not saying don't eat them but know your sensitivity level to determine how safe it is for you. For some people, there is no choice, and you must buy it from a grocery store. If you genuinely want organically grown produce, find a farmer, and ask them detailed questions about their process. You need to know how long the ground has been synthetic fertilizer and pesticide free, what do they do for weed control, how they manage pests, and what they wash the fruits and vegetables with after harvesting them.

Meat

As for organic meat, regulations require that animals are raised in living conditions accommodating their natural behaviors (like the ability to graze on pasture), fed 100-percent organic feed and forage, and not administered antibiotics or hormones.

The reality for most Hidden Consumers is they have various sensitivities to how the meat was butchered and packaged. For those who are vegan, vegetarian, or plant-based, their issues with "organic" meat have more to do with living conditions of the animals or they are on a meat-free diet for health concerns and conditions.

Processed and Multi-Ingredient Food

When it comes to processed, multi-ingredient foods, the 2024 USDA organic standards specify additional considerations. Regulations prohibit organically processed foods from containing artificial preservatives, colors, or flavors and require that their ingredients are organic, with some minor exceptions. For example, processed organic foods may contain some approved non-agricultural ingredients, like enzymes in yogurt, pectin in fruit jams, or baking soda in baked goods.

These definitions are for those who want the USDA Certified Organic label on their package. It does not mean all products that carry this label are 100-percent organic. In processed foods, the requirement is that 70 percent of the ingredients need to be organic.

I can occasionally find safe-ish foods in the bulk section area, but it can still be a struggle. For example, rice was a staple in my diet, as I was eating it three times a day until our move to California. When the grocery stores I used stopped selling a brand of rice I found safe, I tried the bulk section. At the grocery store, it was a no-go. But at Mississippi Market, a co-op, I was fine. I don't know why. It should have been the same process, but there was a clear difference in my reaction levels.

We all know companies use the "organic" marketing label without the USDA certification. The USDA also has regulations around this as well. According to the USDA:

- If you make a product and want to claim that it or its ingredients are organic, your final product probably needs to be certified.
- If you are not certified, you must not make any organic claim on the principal display panel or use the USDA organic seal anywhere on the package.
- You may only, on the information panel, identify the certified organic ingredients as organic and the percentage of organic ingredients.

If a company is not certified and does not meet the requirements per ingredient that needs to be certified organic, it cannot use the term "organic." The problem is there are not enough auditing teams to keep the industry honest. I have talked to independent auditors who struggle with clients who refuse to remove the "organic" term when they don't meet the USDA standards.

Plant-Based / Vegan / Vegetarian

Labeling products for meat-free Hidden Consumers can be challenging, especially because these groups are often referred to interchangeably, which they shouldn't be. The biggest difference between these three groups—plant-based, vegans, and vegetarians—are their motivations to move to a meat-free diet.

Plant-Based Consumers

Plant-based consumers generally fall into two categories: those with health concerns and conditions or those with concerns about over-processed ingredients. Both groups see the food industry as poisoning the general food supply to the detriment of the health of the public. The families that I know of who are plant-based shifted to this lifestyle because of a heart attack, obesity, or diabetes.

This group, no matter why they are plant-based, focuses on their health, and looks for plant-based whole foods. A great example is how they make or buy burgers made from beans, mushrooms, or vegetables. They carefully read labels for ingredients and calorie counts. Most understand the higher the calories and the more refined the ingredients, the more harm that item will cause the body.

There are people in this group who may not be fully committed to going meatless. Their main concern is foods with a lot of highly processed ingredients. They might buy products based on marketing, such as a plant-based burger even though it has cheese on it, or if the bun uses egg.

Vegans and Vegetarians

Vegans and vegetarians are similar in motivation. Both groups focus on animal cruelty and are compassionate towards all animals. The difference between them is the extent of their measures. Vegans are extreme. They eat no animal by-products. No cheese, eggs, honey, etc.

Vegetarians go meat-free, but they might still consume cheese or honey or other animal by-products.

Their diets vary slightly, but they may not be as concerned about the over-processed ingredients in food as the plant-based consumer. The 90's and 00's saw an increase in faux meat products geared to these groups of consumers. Their consumer market for these imitation meat products was the beginning of bioengineering our food.

There are no official or approved definitions for either group. The people who represent this collective group look to outside sources like Dr. T. Collin Campbell and Dr. Neal Bernard, to help them understand and support their journey. From the USDA side, people in these categories are more likely to look for the USDA Organic Certification or other independent sources of certification, to accurately maintain their lifestyle of being meat-free.

Vegans, vegetarians, and plant-based groups share the same characteristic of eating no meat. They share a similar lifestyle even though their motivation is different. Plant-based consumers could be classified as either vegan or vegetarian depending on how extreme they choose to take the new lifestyle.

Bioengineered Ingredients

Let's start with defining a bioengineered ingredient. The USDA fact sheet "What Is a Bioengineered Food?" gives us this definition: Food that contains genetic material that has been modified through certain laboratory techniques and for which the modification could not be obtained through conventional breeding or found in nature.[24]

They go on to say these foods must include a disclosure on the package or label. The other key takeaway is the BE food labels are for marketing purposes only. They don't need to state health or safety concerns.

So, what does "derived from bioengineering or ingredients derived from a bioengineering source" mean? The fact sheet states this: "In this case, the company has chosen to disclose that they are using highly refined ingredients that do not contain detectable modified genetic material in the finished product."

The fascinating fact is these products are not limited to prepackaged products. It also includes fresh fruit and vegetables. As someone who only shops at my farmers' market, I was not aware that bioengineered foods were in the produce department. If you are shopping, look for the BE symbol that stands for "Bioengineered."

In my work with companies that produce bioengineered ingredients, we help them to ensure they are getting the word out on your product. The

USDA has specific guidelines on how to communicate each product's use of bioengineered ingredients:

- The label must have a "contains a bioengineered food ingredient" phrase on the label.
- A symbol in black and white or color stating it is a bioengineered product.
- An electronic or digital link like a QR code to disclose the information.
- A phone number for consumers to get more information.

We use these standards as well to work with brands on marketing to the consumer looking for your products. This includes updates to a brand's website to ensure compliance with all disclosure requirements. We use the Agricultural Marketing Service to ensure proper compliance with the latest rules and regulations. We do take the stance that if you are not sure about disclosure, then you need to disclose the information. We prefer to be safe rather than sorry.

Right now, many consumers do not know or understand what "bioengineered" means. The symbol that food manufacturers and retailers are required to use has been around since January 1, 2022. I did not hear a lot of discussion on the topic from consumers until August of 2023. Why the turn towards bioengineering our food? The simple answer is they are cheaper to make. These products are made from GMOs. My guess is that they are primarily made from GMO corn. Items that are currently approved for availability in bioengineered form are: alfalfa, apples (artic varieties) canola, corn, cotton, eggplant, papaya, pineapple, potato, salmon, soybean, squash, sugar beets, and sugarcane.

The con to bioengineered foods is they are highly processed. If we have learned anything from the research around processed and ultra-processed foods, it is the higher the refinement the higher potential of danger. Foods that are highly refined tend to be lower in nutrients and higher in calories. This can lead to all the potential health risks we discussed under the category of the health-related Hidden Consumer.

The pro is this food will be cheap. You should hopefully be able to save enough on cheap food to cover your healthcare costs. Of course, not everyone can afford food that is not highly refined or processed, which will eventually lead to other economic issues.

Plant-Based Meats

Like bioengineered products, plant-based meats are made from GMOs. They also use processed and highly refined ingredients that deplete nutrients and increase caloric count. The potential dangers of these meats can be seen in the research being done on other highly refined ingredients. They lack nutrients and are high in calories. As any Hidden Consumer can tell you, if you want to reduce calories, you need to look for whole ingredients and less-processed production methods.

Labeling Regulations

The USDA does offer some regulations around how food can be labeled for these groups. Here are some examples from the USDA given to help the industry understand the required auditing standards. Some of these "guidelines" are voluntary. In June of 2024, the USDA launched an effort to "strengthen substantiation of animal-raising claims" in a press release. "The US Department of Agriculture (USDA) announced today that it is implementing a multi-step effort aimed at strengthening the substantiation of animal-raising claims. This action builds on the significant work USDA has already undertaken to protect consumers from false and misleading labels and to implement President Biden's Executive Order on Promoting Competition in the American economy."[25]

It goes on to say that animal-raising claims are voluntary marketing claims and must be approved by USDA FSIS before they can be included on the package. The issue being addressed is whether the current regulations meet the needs and accurately depict the claims being made. Here are the current standards:

- **Grass-Fed and Free-Range:** Animals ate nothing but grass or foraged their entire lives. Also known as "pasture raised."
- **Grain-Fed:** Animals fed grain-based diet a majority of their life. These grains include barley, canola, corn, flax, mixed grain, oat, rye, sorghum, soybean, sunflower, triticale, and wheat.

- **Pasture-Raised:** Grazed in pastures for a minimum of 120 days within each 1-year period.
- **Corn-Fed:** A diet of corn from start to finish.
- **Corn-Finished:** Fed grass and fed corn and byproducts in the last six months.

As for me, this labeling, when used correctly, helps me navigate my food purchases. I eat only free-range or grass-fed meat. There is no bacon or pork in my world since they are always fed corn either in the form of table scraps or actual feed. Animal feed is usually made from feed corn (GMO corn) not sweet corn. Humans eat sweet corn while field corn is not edible and is fed to animals. Not everyone has access to a rancher who ethically raises animals. It is a benefit of living in California to have a wider variety of meat to choose from when you need to get your nutrients from sources that are not vitamins and supplements.

MILLENNIAL CONSUMERS

The Millennial Consumer spends money only if it is worth the investment. They won't buy a product just to have it. If your product can demonstrate or prove a positive impact, you are more likely to gain their business.

The wine industry is a great example of a group worried about the lack of sales to Millennials. A common question is, "How do we engage the Millennial consumer?" One of the issues within the industry is the belief by consumers that the industry is bad for the environment. They see a heavy carbon footprint, water waste, and potential links to soil pollution through pesticides and fertilizers.

The vineyards and wineries who are moving towards a more sustainable future are gaining a foothold with these consumers. They are authentically marketing themselves and discussing issues they see and publicly share how they are solving the problem.

One vineyard where I was a club member talked about the efforts they were putting in to reduce water usage and increase their ability to recycle water. They collected water used for one process and used that water for a different process. Part of their need to do this may have been due to new

California regulations, but it is still a benefit that they could market and show their effort in water conservation.

This group of consumers are also savvy when it comes to researching before buying a product. They read reviews, and they look into a company's background and whom they support politically. All of these factors, and more, are part of their decision-making process. The Millennial Consumer journey is remarkably close to the Hidden Consumer journey. The difference between the two? It's *much easier* to market to Millennials than to Hidden Consumers.

THE FUTURE IS HERE: AI IN MARKETING

The future of marketing leads to additional concerns from all consumers, not just the Hidden Consumers. The main conversations currently surround bioengineered ingredients, plant-based meats, and especially AI marketing. Bioengineered ingredients and plant-based meats are concerns because of how the ingredients are being processed, while AI marketing may lead to an increase in false marketing claims. The other concern in AI marketing is the global effect.

Artificial Intelligence has had legal guidance around it since 2022. However, in 2023 it hit the market for everyone to access. In the world of marketing, especially in the natural and organics communities, I need to know at a minimum how the law impacts my company's work. From the USDA to FDA to the FTC, there are regulations around what can be said in marketing and what cannot be done.

One of my strategic partners is a lawyer in the industry. I have gained a lot of knowledge on the legal side of what I do by working with her. As someone who naturally does not trust AI, I am still keeping up to date on it. I find my conversations on what it can do with her eye-opening. AI is already violating a majority of laws in all areas of the marketing industry. Many companies trust their marketing teams, internal and external, to follow industry guidelines. But since AI is new and shiny, many are ignoring marketing laws to use AI.

The Hidden Consumer already does not trust a majority of the marketing in the industry. We know the tactics used to sway a purchase that could lead to the death of us or a family member. Hidden sugars alone can cause a run to the emergency room. This means transparency in marketing is highly valued. AI takes away transparency. It creates marketing based on what it thinks are the key terms and needs of consumers. I look at the EU's law as an example of the next generation of marketing problems we are facing. The EU's AI Act prohibits specific activities for the use of AI and marketing.

For example, if your company sells products around the world, you need to be aware of the legal restrictions on how you can use AI. Here is a breakdown of the information from the EU Artificial Intelligence Act of 2024.

In summary, the EU has labeled some AI systems as "prohibited" from use. These AI systems are those that use deceptive techniques, impair informed decision-making, or cause significant harm. They exploit vulnerabilities, use biometric categorization systems, use social scoring, use profiling to determine an individual's risk to committing criminal offenses, scrap images from sources to compile facial recognition databases, or use "real-time" remote biometric identification in publicly accessible spaces for law enforcement.

There are also AI systems classified as high-risk. Systems are always considered high-risk if they profile people like in automated processing of personal data to assess aspects of a person's life. High-risk systems fall into current EU laws in Annex I and Annex III. If a company is using a high-risk system, there is a list of requirements a provider must comply with, such as have a risk management system and conduct data governance.

AI systems created for general purposes also have regulations around them. General Purpose AI (GPAI) are systems designed with the capability to serve a variety of purposes. They can be for both direct use and integration with other AI systems. If a GPAI works with a high-risk system, it needs to follow laws for the high-risk AI system. Providers of GPAI systems need to have technical documentation, provide technical documentation to downstream providers, respect the copyright directive, and fully disclose detailed summary about the content used for training the system. The law goes into free and open license GPAI models as well. There are also conditions around notifying the Commission within a specific timeframe if a system meets specific criteria. As part of the codes of practice, it accounts for international approaches and will cover, but not be limited to, the uses listed in the law.

The governance and implementation of the AI Act is through a newly established AI Office. There are processes in place for downstream providers to file complaints against upstream providers. The AI office can also conduct evaluations of the GPAI model, assess compliance, and investigate systematic risk.

One of the areas mentioned in the AI Act is an "open AI system." There are two types of AI: open or closed. Open systems are on a scale of openness; the free systems you can use are typically wide open for anyone to use. They depend on a variety of people to train the system.

Closed systems require a pre-defined interface. Technically, Google and Facebook are closed AI systems. You must use their interface to use their product. The better example is an AI system you must pay to use. The pro for the user is they are less likely to infringe on intellectual property laws. I said earlier I do not trust AI. Part of that is the infringement on my intellectual property. I do not use AI for my business in ways that would take away my right to a thought or idea that originated from me. If I need to reword a sentence that anybody would use, that's when I go to AI for suggestions. But I never use it verbatim.

The other issue with AI is that it relies on traditional search engine optimization (SEO) tactics which I can prove do not work. In my case studies I will delve deeper into this topic. For now, let's dig into how to market to the Hidden Consumer and why these traditional marketing tactics do not work.

3

Marketing To Hidden Consumers

YOU CAN'T EXPECT better results while staying the same.

Every business started somewhere. To achieve success, changes had to be made for their constant growth. This includes everything from investing in better software and redefining your target market, to hiring the right people for the job.

The food and beverage industry has generally gone in the wrong direction when it comes to labeling what is in products. "Natural flavors" is a key phrase that does not necessarily mean natural but can be artificial. Government regulations allow this to be possible. For the Hidden Consumer, it means they have no idea what is being used to make the product. If the choice is between taking a risk or not buying, they will choose not to buy. There seems to be a misunderstanding in the food industry about how people shop. How do you dig deeper into how shopping habits are changing? You need to look at numbers as an example of human behavior and ask different questions.

UNDERSTANDING HUMAN BEHAVIOR

I spent the first two decades of my working life in retail management and customer service where I learned about human behavior and customer needs along the way. This information allowed me to better help my customers then and build better website user flows today.

In retail management, my first big test was a store at the Mall of America. I was promoted to our region's anchor store. It was performing poorly and had only squeaked out $500,000 the previous year. And with rent for the space at $1 million, it wasn't a surprise that the day my district manager handed me the keys she told me I would be receiving a severance package. Their plan was to close the store in 6 months. I gave back the keys two years later. The store was trending towards being an $8 million dollar store.

This did not happen overnight. I had to work hard analyzing various reports and data, like the P&L, watch the interaction between guests and employees, and track stock shipments from receiving to placement on the sales floor. This store failed all around. It needed an overhaul from the backroom to client interaction. The team that stayed and the people who joined the team made it happen. I guided them, trained them, and set up systems to make the process easier. But I also gave my team the power to make recommendations, which led to our success. None of this would have happened if I had not been able to understand our customer's behavior and create systems that helped them shop.

One area where we made this happen was the setup of our backstock area. We had a small area where we kept additional sizes we did not have on the floor. But our time to check to see if we had an extra size was roughly 5 to 10 minutes. We divided the folded area into type and size. One shelf would be small sizes, the next for medium, and so on. On each shelf we had a designated area for blouses, V-necks, sweaters, etc. The top shelves were reserved for shoe backstock. We reduced our backstock checks to a time limit of 30 seconds tops. The difference is customer satisfaction also led to increased sales. They did not have to sit around and wait for the answer. If we had the item, they would buy it. If we didn't, we could easily order it. This also freed up the sales associates' time to go on to help the next customer more quickly.

I have always put my emphasis on the end user. In a brick and mortar, this person can be the employee or the guest. What experience do they want? What are they looking for? What questions do they need answered? If you can answer these questions, you will have taken the first steps to leveling up your business. In the example above, the new system helped both internal and external end user.

Today I use the same analytical ability to build qualified traffic to my client's websites. I understand the shopping habits of the Hidden Consumer who is being underserved. I know the keys to helping you earn part of the $19 billion in sales left on the table each year. My goal is to help my clients refine their ideal client language. It also brings in the Hidden Consumer who wants to buy your product but is not willing to risk buying it without more information. Just like in a brick and mortar, the faster you can give the potential client what they want or need, the faster you can close a sale and serve the next person. The beauty is that we also create language and copy that can be used on **all** marketing platforms from website to digital marketing to traditional marketing. I created my own Signature System to focus on identifying the Hidden Consumer for each client—and it's a system you can apply to your own brand.

THE HIDDEN CONSUMER SIGNATURE SYSTEM

Before I jump into any project, I like to start with an assessment looking at the health of your website, how you show up online in all areas, if the language on your website makes a connection to your ideal consumer, and where at a glance we will need to create wording around product ingredients. I also like to estimate how many, if any, new site pages might need to be created for a brand and evaluate a brand's categories, tags, and e-commerce setup if a brand sells online.

We also pull out our business analysis tool kit. This gives us a clear understanding of communication within your organization. We want our full process to go as smoothly as possible. This requires us to know who we need to talk to in each department and who has final decision-making power, otherwise known as RACI (Responsible, Accountable, Consult, Inform). Our work is only as good as the communication system that is in place, which is why we also need to know what software a brand uses for internal and external communication. Our assessment sets everyone up for a successful working relationship.

These are few of the Business Analysis tools I use when assessing a brand's approach to reaching Hidden Consumers:

- Needs Assessment
- RACI (Responsible, Accountable, Consult, Inform)
- Goals and Objectives
- SWOT Analysis and SWOT Strategy
- Interrelationship Diagram
- Weighted-Ranking Matrix (if software is needed)

We believe it is important to document our work and loop people in where they are needed. Our clients and their teams are busy. If they want a quick process, we need to be on the same page with what needs to be done. We will propose a timeline, but the reality is if the client does not make our work a priority, then the work will drag on. Once we have an assessment completed and discussed with those in charge, we move on to bringing in the Hidden Consumer.

How do you market to people who are "hidden"? This group may seem elusive, but the reality is you know someone or many "someones" in these groups. People who have issues with food are so commonplace, we overlook them. The other factor here is how quickly these groups have grown in numbers. They are no longer the minority of people, but the majority. Here is a look at what you need to help your brand reach the Hidden Consumer:

- **Phase 1: Attract, Engage, and Convert** is focused on quick results. The website is the root of success. Our system creates a solid foundation for continually increased numbers that do not require constant supervision. Our branding and marketing specialist is working with your marketing team to ensure your message is consistent across all platforms.
- **Phase 2: The Hidden Markets** phase brings focus into the new markets we find for our clients. Who is searching for your product

FIGURE 3-1

Hidden Consumers
C O N S U L T I N G

ATTRACT, ENGAGE, CONVERT	HIDDEN MARKETS	INTERNAL CLIENTS
SIMPLY HIDDEN ASSESSMENT	**INGREDIENT TRANSPARENCY**	**SYSTEMS IN PLACE & SOPS**
User experience Brand voice Tech health	Breakdown of ingredients	Automations Back-up systems
IMMEDIATE WEBSITE IMPLEMENTATION	**HIDDEN MARKET OUTREACH**	**TRAINING**
User experience Copy Data	Marketing on all channels Hidden consumer groups	Marketing Sales Purchasing
RESULTS	**RESULTS**	**RESULTS**
Organic Traffic Engagement Time User Flow	Organic Traffic Engagement Time Sales	Traffic Engagement Time Sales

HIDDEN IN PLAIN SIGHT: CONNECTING WITH ELUSIVE OR UNTAPPED CONSUMER BASE

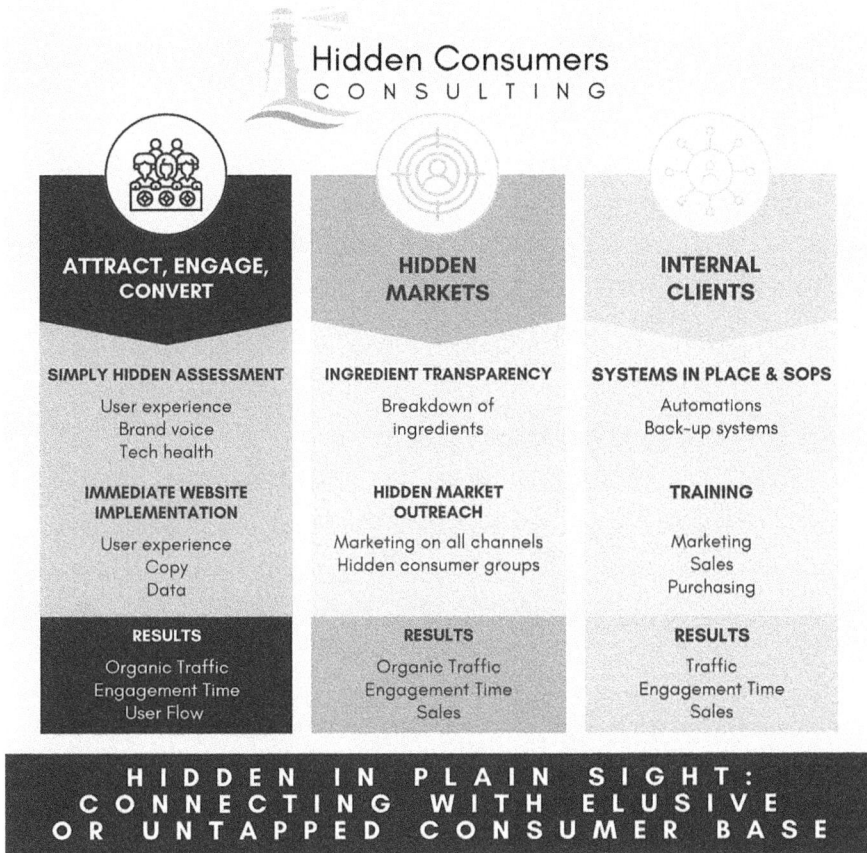

but not finding you? Our team is refining your copy and finding where your Hidden Consumer is hanging out. The branding and marketing specialist is working with your marketing team to create a strategy that talks to these consumers.

- **Phase 3: The Internal Client** phase is where we set up the backend processes and systems so you can maintain what we have created. We start with what software you use. We integrate what needs to be done with your software. Automations are important to ensure continual communication with all parties involved.

As you can see, the branding and marketing portion of this system is about ensuring you are consistent across all platforms with your message.

When I'm working with a client, I provide branding updates such as new logo design and new packaging to a full marketing strategy to embrace all the consumers looking for your brand. At the same time, we also look at your claims. Do you have the right certifications in place to claim "organic" or "dairy-free" or even "vegan." We need to see the full picture from the consumer perspective to better understand how to bring in the Hidden Consumer. The goal is to ensure that consumers stop and read your message.

Each of these three pieces work like gears. If one section is not functioning, it shuts down the whole process. Let's dig deeper into each phase of work.

THE CORE OF SUCCESS: ATTRACT, ENGAGE, AND CONVERT

There seems to be a general belief that if you build a website and make it pretty, your ideal client will find you and just buy from you as if by magic. It's almost a "build it and they will come" mentality. This type of strategy will make you believe websites are not important because they generate no leads or sales for you. The other side is how you track results and understand what good numbers look like for your website.

Our process starts with a website assessment and a branding and marketing assessment. It does not matter what industry you are in. We've created user-friendly websites for sustainable landscaping, real estate, coaching and consulting, artists and art dealers, natural food, and food industry auditors, to name a few. In every industry, the website was the key to their continued success. Even if your site is only for referral traffic, it still needs to perform like a passive salesperson.

In the food and beverage industries, it is imperative to have a website that is user friendly and authentic if you want a piece of the $19-billion-dollar+ pie. Here are the key areas we look at and questions we ask while going over each client's website to make sure it's optimized for the Hidden Consumer:

1. **Discuss how your ingredients are made.** What does the company who makes your ingredients use to make something like dextrose or citric acid? Explain what is in "natural ingredients."

2. **Discuss what ingredients you use and why.** If you choose truly natural and organic ingredients, why do you choose them? I have worked with people at many wonderful companies who are making products with ingredients sourced specifically for their quality, but that info is nowhere on the website. Don't hide your attention to details. Celebrate it.

3. **Each product should list the type of packaging it comes in.** The unfortunate side of the increased focus on "recyclable plastics" is more people are allergic to them. Plastics for food and beverages are food grade. This means they are made from GMO corn. Those of us with a corn sensitivity (estimated to be around 2 million people minimum) need to avoid these plastics. Not to mention there is no truly recyclable plastic, and this is partially where nano plastics in humans come from.

4. **Website accessibility is also important for all sites in all industries.**
   a. Look at color contrasts. I had a client who used five shades of blue for her logo. That means, 300 million people cannot see beyond the basic outline of the logo. The other issue was the use of light blue text on dark blue backgrounds. Tone on tone cannot be seen by those with various levels of colorblindness.
   b. Beyond the color contrasts, make sure ALT text is in place, links are named, and each page has description relevant to that page's topic.
   c. We do not have the ability to make sites 100-percent compliant on our own, but we will get the basics in place. To meet compliance standards, we offer an ADA plugin. The problem with the plugin is it does not write ALT text, and it does not name links or write authentic descriptions for pages. My work plus the plugin does create fully compliant websites.

5. **Mobile load speed is also important.**
   a. According to Faverio, one in three Americans shops with their mobile device weekly. This means a lot of money is being left on the table if your website doesn't speak to your ideal client and doesn't load in under 3.8 seconds.

b. According to the Think with Google report from 2019, "75% of smartphone users expect to get immediate information while using their smartphone." You might be one of those who walks away from a website that won't load fast enough. What is the parameter for "fast enough"? It is 3.8 seconds according to Google Performance Reports. Most sites load at an average of 7 seconds. This means most people are not seeing your website if it loads slower than their expectation. You will want to know what is stopping your site from loading on most people's devices. This means taking a look at your webhost and elements you use on each page.

c. Design trends currently are the number one reason servers struggle to load websites. Most designers don't use numbers to determine the best design. Case in point: If you go to almost any website of a small business you will see on the first screen or top of the fold, a hero image or video. This is matched with one to two buttons saying, "Schedule now!" and "Learn more!" which a human doesn't actually click on.

d. Every element on a page must load. At the top of every page the image or video has to load, plus the text box, then the text, then the button, the text on the button, then the link for the button, then another button and its elements, the logo, the navigation menu with links, the heading box, and the heading text, and so on. Even though most of these steps can be done in a split second, it does add up.

e. What if you fix the content and copy and are drawing the right traffic to your site but you see no change in engagement? Your site is not loading for most people. Did you know it takes a video used as a header a minimum of 4 seconds to load? Just the video. You block users to your site by having a video at the top of the page. Buttons can take up to 3 seconds to load. The more buttons you have the longer the load time.

The best part of implementing these steps is you will authentically increase your SEO. Say you have a product that you deliberately made nut-free because you or someone you love is allergic. You went through the steps of creating or using a nut-free facility. You sourced each ingredient to ensure no cross-contamination. But all you tell people is, "It's nut free!" You are missing out on key organic traffic.

Your website could have a category or sub-category of food labeled "nut free" based on your product line. Your landing page for this category would start out with the why and how you can claim that label. If you are truly looking at cross-contamination, you are most likely doing more than what is federally required. State that fact and show what you did versus the minimum requirements of the FDA. But beware. If you lie, you are setting yourself up for litigation.

This does not need to be a long section, and it should not be a long section. After this description you will want to list each product that falls under that label. You have now created a page that helps search engines direct qualified traffic to you, but you have also created a site that focuses on the user and makes it easy for people to buy SAFE products from you. The consumer is happy with you and your product, and they switch to buying only your product. They also recommend you to everyone, especially those in their same food aversion groups. **Plus,** you get word of mouth referrals in the Hidden Consumer communities. It's a win-win for you.

But how do you know it worked? This is where your website data is key. Here are the questions you need to ask for your data.

1. **How many users visited your site?**
   When assessing user traffic, use windows of the last 30 days, quarter-to-date, year-to-date, and comparison to the previous year. This helps track if you are on the right path to bringing in an increase in users.

2. **How much of your traffic was organic versus direct versus referral versus overall numbers?**
   If your organic traffic numbers are increasing across most search engines it means search engines are seeing a change in what you are looking for in user traffic and sending you more people.

3. **How engaged were users overall versus organic traffic?**
   This is a time tracking question. Any engagement time under

30 seconds means something is wrong. You can also use this number to verify if the person who wants your product is being shown your site. The higher the engagement time, the higher the likelihood of your ideal client finding you. On average, my clients see a minimum engagement time of 1 minute and 30 seconds.

4. **What pages were in the top 10 and bottom 10? What products ranked higher?**
   This is key to understanding where you have copy that is engaging (if that page's time meets minimum standards) or where you need to rework the copy to increase engagement.

5. **Did a product that should rank higher not get enough visibility and engagement?**
   This is key if you have a new product that is being launched. You want to understand how it was received or if you were able to quickly find the ideal market for it. These numbers will determine your next strategy. If it all looks good, you will keep going and put in place the steps you planned. If it's not good, you will need to re-evaluate what to do and determine the root cause of the problem.

6. **Retention. How many users came back? There should be a minimum of 10 percent return.**
   Overall, a minimum of 10 percent of your organic traffic should be returned to your website. The higher the retention percentage rate, the more likely you are to find new brand-loyal customers.

An additional data source is your customer service department. You should be tracking more than the number of calls and complaints, asking the following questions:

1. **What questions do consumers have?**
   You should have categories that calls can easily be placed into such as ingredient questions, company questions, allergy questions, and a category for questions that are unclear.

2. **What ingredient questions are being asked for more details?**
   Specifically, what are customers asking about? How many times do people ask how your dextrose or citric acid are made?

3. **How are your people trained to reply to these questions?**
   What is your company's response to the questions? This is the key to understanding whether people will trust you or not.
4. **Did your AI chatbot effectively answer the question or incite fury?**
   In general, you should be tracking what your AI is answering and how they answer questions. Also have in place similar categories to when people are calling into your customer service team.

The first company we worked with in the industry was a tomato chip company with farms in Mexico. They make tomato chips by picking them fresh off the vine and freeze drying them. These chips also came in different flavors. We were not hired to help them understand the ingredients. We were hired by a group of investors for our Attract, Engage, and Convert method. Their goal was to launch the product line on Amazon. Amazon stores are not something we work on, but we could help with keywords and the website.

The website work included creating a new homepage that focused on their natural and organic products. The sales portion was linked to their Amazon Store. We focused on meta descriptions and copy for the pages and products. In the process of researching keywords, we also realized they had a hidden consumer market. This was the beginning of me putting the Hidden Consumer Signature System together.

At the time, I was not calling these groups of markets Hidden Consumers. This came into creation as I started embracing my new direction. But the Tomato Chip Company was the beginning of me seeing the potential of what we could do, and it all starts with the website. Once you have your website set up to connect with buyers, then you can move into the next phase.

REACHING THE HIDDEN MARKET

We use this second phase to tighten up the language on different pages and products. If your product is truly GF but you are not using it as marketing strategy, work it in. The reality is many companies misuse the phrase "gluten-free" when they are not. Our food industry is truly "buyer beware." This also means if you are not truly GF, we will recommend the language be removed or that you go through the process to become GF certified if you want to use a GF label.

The ability to bring in the Hidden Consumer market starts with your website, as I've already mentioned. Setting up categories and subcategories based on different Hidden Consumers will help you achieve success faster, but you need to do more for the next level of growth. The Hidden Market phase is about refining your marketing strategy based on who is looking for you. Frankly, this is my favorite part of my work. I like to start with the person who you know wants your product and then refine it based on who we have identified as new groups to help bring in new lines of revenue.

My team usually finds new consumer markets throughout the first phase of work. Our work with the Tomato Chip Company discovered three additional consumer groups they could market too. One group we found was a subculture of people who loved all things made from tomatoes. This meant their tomato chips were not just for people wanting a healthier option to potato chips. We also felt they could reach more people if they explained what was in "natural flavors."

They were the first natural and organic client we worked with in the food and beverage industry. I asked them what was in "natural flavors." I don't remember the ingredients, but I do remember it was only one item. I did ask them, "Why don't they just say that on the label?"

If you look at their ingredients today, you can see they stepped away from being "natural" and "organic." The amount of lab-created ingredients in their products has expanded their ingredients list from five or so items to a laundry list. One issue could be the focus on Amazon sales. True natural and organic products will have a limited shelf life; therefore, they will not be sellable where you need long shelf life for warehouses and distribution. The new ingredients are preservatives to enhance the longevity of their products.

Due to issues between the investors and the company who owned the rights to the tomato chips, my team and I were let go over funding cuts. We were not able to move onto the next steps of helping market the strengths of their brand. One of these strengths we would have focused on was the minimal ingredients.

All of this means that we were not able to perfect their outreach to the Hidden Consumers we had identified. They had to fall back on old marketing tactics to grow the product quickly and within Amazon's framework. Had we started with the project at an earlier level, we might have seen a different outcome.

Had we moved forward, our next steps would have been to set up the back-end systems and automation to ensure their marketing stayed on track to reach the Hidden Consumer.

INTERNAL CLIENTS

The biggest factor in a company's continued success is training and standard operating procedures (SOPs). The education of internal employees, from the top down, to understand the changing environment and buying habits of consumers is where your hidden revenue lives. From a procedure standpoint, the more we can automate, the less work we place on the teams.

The reality is my company is working on SOPs and training from day one. Our goal is to make an impact and get your results right away, which we do (organic traffic increases start within 24 hours). My average client sees a 300-percent increase in organic traffic in the first four weeks. But those numbers are not fully sustainable without maintaining your transparency.

Training

We start documenting what information each department needs to do their job. Let's use the sales and marketing departments as an example. The biggest legal issue companies face is making false claims about the products. It is easy for a marketing department to claim "sugar-free" because they do not see the word "sugar" in the list of ingredients. I am going to give them the benefit of the doubt and say they may not realize "dextrose" or "ethyl maltol" are hidden sugars. A person with diabetes may realize this and not buy your product. They will also lose any trust they have in your company. Those who may be new to a diabetes diagnosis may not realize all the names that sugars go by. They may not know the danger they are in until their next checkup, which again leads to a loss of trust in your company and a word-of-mouth reputation that is less than desirable.

What we do is document the key training that will be needed by each department. We are also creating SOP's that work with multiple departments, so everyone is on the same page.

Standard Operating Procedures

When it comes to ingredients, multiple departments need to be kept in the loop when it comes to changes. As part of the assessment, I talked about earlier, by this point, you will have already determined how many people need to be kept on top of what information.

The groups below typically need to be notified, though your organization may have some variation on what is listed:

- **Sales and Marketing** needs to alter how they talk about the product to potential buyers.
- **Ingredient Purchasing** needs to be aware of what is being used in products. (This may not be relevant in all companies.)
- **Customer Service** will need to update the teams to ensure accurate information is being relayed when consumers call or chat with them.
- **Human Resources**, specifically those in charge of training, will need to update any of the training documents to ensure new employees are on the same page as everyone else when they start.
- **Legal** will need to be notified in case changes need to be made to any legal statements around the products.

Your company needs to be able to quickly communicate with consumers when changes happen.

On April 12, 2023, *The Washington Post* ran an article with a misleading headline, but the issue discussed was just as serious. The headline of the article "To Comply with A New Sesame Allergy Law, Some Businesses are Adding Sesame" was false. Businesses were not adding sesame to their products *because* of the law. However, the law did help bring into the light all the products that were using sesame.

What the law does is mandate careful cleaning to prevent cross-contamination, legally require ingredient transparency, and set standards for legal amounts of sesame that can be in products. This means by January 1, 2023, businesses **had to** disclose all the ways they use sesame that could be harmful to those with sensitivities and allergies.

This article focused on moms who were shocked to find out sesame was used in Wendy's hamburger buns. One mom even said Wendy's had been the only safe fast food she could take her kids to. The moms in this article believed Wendy's deliberately put sesame in the buns after the law went into effect instead of focusing on cleaning the equipment the buns were made on.

My hot take is I don't believe the law made them decide to start using more sesame. What the industry had been doing leading up to the law was making a move to add more sesame in products in lieu of cleaning the machinery, which might have forced the law into being due to cases being reported.

It may have been purely coincidence the law went into effect as Wendy's vendor was able to make the switch. Reality is only the vendor and Wendy's knows the truth. However, this story does demonstrate a much larger problem in the food industry: the lack of communication between businesses and consumers who are trying to keep themselves safe.

When a business or their vendor changes an ingredient, informing the consumer **should be** the next step. But this is not something that can be done by snapping your fingers. What this story illustrates is how important it is for multiple departments to communicate with each other. Marketing should have been brought in to clearly discuss with consumers how Wendy's was complying with federal law. If your company still runs on a silo mentality, you are killing your bottom line.

The scenario that should have happened at Wendy's is this (I do not know what the actual process was, but based on information available, the below steps did not fully happen):

1. Bun manufacturer notifies Wendy's for FDA compliance. At this point, Wendy's should already have in place an SOP with each vendor on how to communicate ingredient changes.
2. The point person or department notifies each correlating department of the changes.

3. Each department rolls out their department specific SOPs:
    a. **Marketing:** SOPs consist of notifying consumers of changes to ingredients.
    b. **Sales:** Notifies each sales representative of the changes and updates sales pitch.
    c. **Customer Service:** Documentation updated to accurately relay the message through customer calls and chats.
    d. **Legal:** Needs to be notified to be aware of what potential threats will need to be handled.

The timeline for this will depend on when your company can expect the new ingredient to be used in their products. If this is an "oops" on the side of the manufacturer, you now need to go into risk management mode and relay the information as soon as possible. If this is a notification of your future batch number that will include or not include this ingredient, it can be rolled out based on the schedule. It will need to still be a priority, but not an "in 24 hours" priority.

Your company's SOPs may vary. Factors that alter this example include making your own ingredients, buying ingredients but making the product yourself.

Wendy's misstep happened when sesame became an FDA-recognized allergen, and their bun manufacturers had to declare sesame seeds and oil in their products. This key information was not fully communicated to Wendy's customers. If it had been, it would not have made the news.

Let's take a look at how the different departments should be working together for ingredient transparency.

Ingredient Purchasing / Product Manager

This person or team is the key to how you market your product. They should receive information from the ingredient manufacturer or from the company making your product on how each ingredient is made. An overview of this information needs to be sent onto marketing and sales of what they cannot or can say about the product. For example, a product that includes alternative types of sugars cannot be labeled "sugar-free."

The customer service team needs to have their files updated on the ingredients as well. Each sugar alternative used should be listed with how it was made to accurately answer consumer questions. For example, dextrose is derived from moldy corn. There may be people who are sensitive to the mold and/or corn in this ingredient.

Marketing and Sales

Did you know there are legal requirements around how you can market your products? You cannot make claims like "sugar-free" if you have added sugar alternatives. The problem is roughly 90 percent of products on the market violate this law. So often, it comes down to marketing teams not understanding or knowing how ingredients are made.

Human Resources

The training department will need to be notified if updates need to be made to training materials. This is imperative to ensure all employees are on the same page.

Customer Service

In the early days of learning about allergies and sensitivities, the Hidden Consumer would trust a company's customer service team to understand how a product is made. They do this with horrible effects on their health. It's all too common for new people learning to navigate their allergies to end up in the emergency room because they were given bad advice or a wrong answer from a company.

They often hear, "It's safe for you to eat our product." Or, "That ingredient won't be found in our product." Or maybe they say, "The proteins are processed out." The Hidden Consumer believes they are getting the right answer. They buy the product and test it and then promptly become ill. The food industry has a reputation amongst veteran Hidden Consumers as being ignorant on the ins and outs of food production from the lab to manufacturing to being sold.

A great example from my early days of learning was vitamin shopping and reading the labels. Today, I know there is no such thing as a safe vitamin or supplement for me. But back then I was still hopeful. I wrongly thought the staff at the vitamin store would know all about corn in products. I was so naive. The salesperson said she knew of one vitamin with absolutely no corn in it because the label said "no corn" and "corn-free." I looked at the label and checked out the ingredients list. **Every single ingredient** was derived from corn. The product may not have been made with cornstarch or corn in another direct ingredient, but for me it was just as unsafe as if it had been. The lack of knowledge from vitamin maker to store employee is normal. This is what people with any level of food sensitivity must go up against daily.

Legal

Each legal department will have their own guidelines on what notifications they need to be notified of and when. If they are a proactive department, they will want to know of changes that affect how the products are discussed for marketing and sales.

THE HIDDEN CONSUMER JOURNEY

What if you could take the people who might buy your product and turn them into brand-loyal customers? It is not as crazy as it sounds. The key is understanding who the Hidden Consumer is and what they are looking for in products. The Hidden Consumer is looking to reduce health risks, avoid specific ingredients, and practice their concern for animals and the environment.

A person who shops based on reading labels is not necessarily reading for calorie count. More people today read labels for ingredients versus nutrition information. What I have noticed is that most stop counting calories. If you start to remove the excess ingredients, you reduce the calories automatically. This is key to understanding the Hidden Consumer journey. They will not just buy the new shiny product sitting on the shelf unless they have already vetted your company.

What exactly are these consumers looking for? Here are the average steps a Hidden Consumer takes before buying a product:

1. **Examine the packaging and marketing for red flags.** Is the company using terms like "sugar-free," but they can clearly see two or more hidden sugars in the ingredients label? Do you claim

"organic," but the website doesn't show details on what organic means or have the needed certifications to back up the claim? Or maybe its "gluten-free" but the product is manufactured in a building with wheat. Roughly 90 percent of products that are on the market have misleading labels.

2. **Read the ingredients list.** Are there any ingredients that need to be avoided? Or does the dreaded "natural flavors" appear? "Natural flavors" are not natural, and this is where companies can legally hide ingredients. Any of the five Hidden Consumer groups will automatically put the product back on the shelf. A great example is high fructose corn syrup (HFCS). The FDA in 2013 declared it a "natural" ingredient meaning it could be labeled as a natural flavor.[26] Around the time I was determining what my allergy was, HFCS was all over the news. Since then, researchers have made connections between health issues and behavior to HFCS. It was around 2015 when we saw the use of HFCS "disappear" from packages. But what really happened is companies hid the ingredients under "natural flavors."

3. **Research the company.** This might happen during Step 1 based on the consumer's level of technology they have access to. The keys the Hidden Consumer is looking for are about transparency. Is the company who they claim to be? How much information do they give consumers on packaging, ingredients, and company values? The next piece is do they walk the talk or is it all a smoke screen? The Hidden Consumer is well-versed in online research and knows how to dig to determine real values versus proclaimed values.

4. **Make the reluctant call to customer service.** If a consumer is genuinely interested in your product but not finding the needed information, they call or chat with customer service. Most with food intolerances to allergies only make these calls in the beginning of their journey. The realization is that no food or beverage company understands the depth of sensitivity that is possible to ingredients, which leads to many Hidden Consumers becoming sick or worse because of a reaction. The number of times I hear or see emails from companies being posted in allergy

communities claiming "there is no way you could be allergic to our products" is disheartening at a minimum. No one should ever claim their products are safe for everyone. Since you cannot be sure why people are buying your product, you need to be able to talk honestly about how your product is made. When a person with an unrecognized allergy calls your customer service department looking for answers on how food ingredients are made, you need to know the answers.

The full process can take hours to months depending on the response time. The consumer may drop the digging and give it up if something else comes along that meets their needs easily. The bottom line is you need to be as transparent as possible, and you will gain their trust faster.

INGREDIENT TRANSPARENCY

The solution is to not only create more sales but also build consistent sales through active ingredient transparency.

Look at your ingredients and how you make that information accessible to consumers. Some of this will come into play when you look at what pages people are looking at. Ask questions similar to: Do you have a dedicated page that talks about your ingredients or is the list of ingredients a drop-down box on the page? Do you have numbers on how many people use the drop-down box?

Look at your sales channels to see if you are reaching your ideal client. What is your marketing strategy to stay connected to those who have shown interest in what you do and your products? If your total time on site is under 10 seconds, you have one of two issues: 1) your site is not attracting the right audience, and they leave your site after seeing the initial page or 2) your site doesn't work on mobile devices. You can determine which one or if it's both by looking at the flow of people off the initial page.

Companies do not understand the extent their Hidden Consumer has to go to find safe products. Once you understand the length people must go to eat safely and not become ill or worse, die, marketing your product becomes easier. When I find a product I can use, I am your consumer until you make a change in packaging or ingredients.

When you do not understand who wants to buy your products, you can't see your full potential. You don't know what Hidden Consumer could be looking for your products. The digital age seems to have created a marketing world that no longer focuses on who will buy your product, but just throw a large net and see who comes in. You may see lots of traffic to your website but no engagement. This leads to low volume sales and even less brand loyalty, which would bring in consistent sales.

As a company, you want as many people to buy your products as possible. The best way to achieve this goal is by thinking about why you created your product, food, or company in general. Did you create a company focused on being different? Did you want to provide a healthier option or even safer option to the public, but no one seems to care? Then you have not discovered how to find your ideal customer or reach the Hidden Consumer. I can tell you from personal experience that it is not because of lack of care that people are not buying your product. It is from not being able to find you in the vastness of the internet.

Traditional SEO is part of this problem. You may have hired a team of people to focus on your keywords, backlinks, and other means to drive traffic to your website, but the results are dismal or it takes **years** to see a meager result. You might have even tried digital ads, but to no avail. The problem is you are focused on the tech and not the person.

When you start to focus on the people who will buy your product, a new strategy develops. They give you the information you need to reach more people like them. Now if in this process you have stumbled upon someone with an allergy, this is what will happen. They are going to check your ingredients and packaging for safeness. Next, one of two things will happen: One, they have enough information to trial your product and buy it right then. Or two, they are going to dig deeper and research you online or contact your customer service department to ask specific questions.

If everything goes well, they get the answers they are looking for and the trial goes well. You have a new brand-loyal customer. The amount of work that goes into finding safe-ish products to trial is daunting in most cases. I know when I find a brand I can eat safely, I buy them every week until the company changes ingredients or packaging of the product.

An example is Simple Mills Sprouted Crackers. I found these crackers and they worked well for a couple of years. But then I started to notice I was reacting. Was it due to eating too many crackers? Was the cracker safe or did I convince myself it had been safe? The ingredients did not seem to change but the packaging did. What happened? The most likely cause was the change in packaging, but I cannot rule out they may have changed a vendor for one ingredient that was corn contaminated.

In this case, I believe the company started using a different supplier for one or more of their ingredients. This new supplier may not have the best practices around how they acquire ingredients, how they enforce cleaning practices, or maybe they make the ingredients based on what's the cheapest source. Either way, this is common practice in the food industry. I am sure for most people they are still safe to eat. But for someone on the super-sensitive side, they no longer are for me, which means I am back to the drawing board to find a safe cracker. I am currently doing well with WASA light rye crackers. We'll see how this goes, but right now it's working for me.

When food is processed instead of grown, you are using ingredients people wouldn't consume in large quantities. Substances like moldy corn are a base for many food ingredients. That soft drink you enjoy? It's basically liquid moldy corn. Does your Hidden Consumer have a mold allergy? They might want to look at their soft drink consumption and associated allergic reactions. Do they drink diet sodas with sweeteners? They are still drinking liquid moldy corn but now also ingest an additive that may alter DNA. But they won't know any of that unless your brand uses transparency when discussing ingredients and labeling products.

DATA FROM HIDDEN CONSUMER CASE STUDIES

I am **still** discovering companies whose product I might be able to use. Some companies have been around longer than I have had to be concerned about how my food or other products are made. The biggest obstacle to finding these products has been their use of traditional SEO. Hidden Consumers are not average web cruisers. They are searching for products with distinct properties, or those that lack specific ingredients. No SEO keyword tool is going to help you connect to them. What it takes is someone with knowledge of how the group of people you want to sell to thinks.

In the past we have worked with a variety of clients from service based to product based. But one common denominator for all is that focusing on the end-user brought in higher results than focusing on Google algorithms. Conversion rates and increased sales all come down to one key factor: Are you answering the users' questions? To understand if you are or are not, you need to understand how to read human behavior in numbers. What the numbers tell me based on the full website or individual pages is whether users are finding value in your website. My process starts with a look at the homepage numbers. Because at the end of the day, humans impact your numbers. If you want better data, focus on the person you need to engage on your website.

One of the statements I hear **all the time** is "no one lands on the homepage." Based on my data, this is false. Every single website I have reviewed, analyzed, or worked on sees the most traffic landing on the homepage first. When many people type a phrase or word into the search engine box, they do not know what they are looking for specifically. This is why knowing your ideal client language is the key to success, not keyword tools. People searching for an answer to their problem will not know the solution they need. This is why search engines send users to the homepage.

From the homepage, I want to know the path people use. My parameters are that a minimum of 50 percent of the people who land on the homepage should move on to another page. If this is not happening, I need to run a performance report and I need to review the content and copy of the homepage. In most cases, the load time and content both need to be resolved to engage more people.

I also look at users and new users, engagement time, engagement rate, retention of new users, and engaged sessions to start. These numbers will give me the needed data to determine next steps and priorities for each site.

Based on conversations with our clients, we want to know how people use their website, what they are or were they looking for. There is a lot of information you glean from seeing which pages people visit and in what order. Do they follow your call-to-action buttons or are they looking for something different? You can use this information to create a more user-friendly website. Let's look at a few case studies that we used these questions in and see the results we achieved for the client.

CASE STUDY 1: Food, Pharma, and Cosmetics Industry Compliance for Federal and State

At the end of 2022, we began working with a company focused on federal and state compliance with standards in the food industry. We are still working with them on various projects, so I will keep most of the information about them to a minimum.

We were hired to help update the website to bring in a specific type of qualified user. They were working on a project that would be the first of its kind. As I write this, the project has not gone live yet but our work did help them get the first 100 users needed for this specific program. We tracked whether we saw an increase in users. Yes, we did. Did those users go to the page the company needed them to go to? Yes, they did. Did the overall engagement time on the website increase? Yes, it did.

The scope of work included: updating the homepage for user flow, updating copy and content, creating new copy discussing the special project, and creating three new pages based on the special project users to reflect each one's different needs. My team identified three distinct users who would need to use this special project.

In November and December of 2022, the company saw 13 users or 6.5 people a month. Only 43 percent, or 5.5 people, were engaged with the site for an average of 37 seconds.

Between January and May of 2023, there had been 228 users or 45 people visiting their website a month. Their engagement rate increased to 89 percent, or 203 people, that were actively using the site.

This was an increase of 1,529 percent in users, and an increase of 68 percent in engagement rate. Sessions started were a total of 326 with 290 engaged sessions. This is an increase of 1818 percent in sessions started. For added fun, the number of engaged sessions per user also increased by 3122 percent.

This is the graph of the breakdown of numbers to give you a clear picture of what we accomplished in the first few months:

Metric	Nov & Dec 2023	Jan to May 2023	% Change
Organic Traffic	13 users 6.5 monthly 14 engaged sessions	228 users 45 monthly 174 engaged sessions	1,529%
Organic Engaged %	43% (5.5 users)	89% (203 users)	68%

When comparing the end of 2022 to early 2023, a majority of our work went live after the first quarter 2023, which explains why the numbers in the 2nd table show only 14 users in the first quarter of 2023.

One year later, their numbers also show significant improvement. Let's look at the first quarter 2023 compared to first quarter 2024.

Metric	1st Quarter 2023	1st Quarter 2024	% Change
Organic Traffic	14 users 14 engaged sessions	132 users 174 engaged sessions	843%, 1,143% engagement increase
Organic Engagement Time	57 seconds	51 seconds	11% decrease Not uncommon with significant increase in traffic
Event Counts	3.88	5.91	53% increase

Here is a breakdown of the top pages between the two quarters.

Top Pages	1st Quarter 2023	1st Quarter 2024	% Change
Home	161 views 96 users	2,345 views 742 users	1,357% increase in views 673% increase in users
Services	60 views 24 users	333 views 1126 users	455 increase in views 425% increase in users
Application Form	28 views 13 users	229 views 92 users	418% increase in views 608% increase in users
About	34 views 16 users	176 views 72 users	418% increase in views 350% increase in users

The third table shows the differences between the same pages one year apart. My team's goal is to focus on each critical page the user needs to decide about working with you or buying your product. What information does the user want and need to make the decision to work with your company? This is the information we added to the copy. The key is how the copy is written to engage the user. It needs to be conversational language that the user can connect to. The application form page is the critical page for conversion. We saw a 608 percent increase in conversion. As the client says, the website is running now.

CASE STUDY 2: Long Term Results with Attract, Engage, and Convert

An e-commerce client came to me at the end of 2020, and we worked together until the end of 2023. They had been on the verge of closing at the end of 2019 and into early 2020. In 2019 most of the big box stores that sold this client's products dropped them from their shelves. Big box stores accounted for around 60 percent of their business. The other issue is small business owners who sell my client's products have seen a sharp decline in sales. A lot of these businesses are permanently closed.

COVID-19 helped this client to stay on their feet and put together a new business strategy. They knew the success of 2020 could not last forever. They had found success by using Etsy and selling their handcrafted items there, but they knew they needed a website that sold their products as well.

Early 2021, I started working with them to build their ecommerce site. At the end of 2021, they had 7,100 users who on average were engaged with the full website for 1 minute. They averaged 645 users a month. Of the 7,100 users, 2229 were from organic searches. We also saw 631 of these visitors returning to the site. But we needed to go deeper into the numbers. Out of the 7,100 only 14.4 percent were engaged with the site, or 1,022 people. BUT the organic search traffic was engaged for an average of 23.29 percent for 2 mins and 42 seconds. Users started 4,596 sessions but only 662 of these sessions were engaged. Meaning only 662 sessions involved clicking, scrolling, or other activity that required an action.

What do the numbers tell us? This site was being built and was a full 11-month project to complete. While building the site, we were able to draw in traffic but not quite qualified traffic to this point. We had focused on a specific ideal client while building the site and the constant updates did keep the site updated in Google Searches. The downside is the constant updates also altered who Google would send to the site as a qualified user. You can see this in the engagement rate numbers. My minimum parameter for my clients is a 50 percent engagement rate. Anything less and we are not bringing in the ideal client, which was the case for the 2021 numbers. At this time, we did not have Google Search Console connected. It was not connected until the end of January 2022.

The client signed a retainer agreement, and we worked together again in 2022 to level up the site.

Numbers for 2022 were good. Total visitors on site were 11,950. They averaged roughly 1,000 users a month. This is an increase of 355 visitors per month over 2021 totals. New users accounted for 1,200 of the total users count with a 10 percent retention rate. They met the minimum parameter for retention. Total website visitors saw an engagement rate of 1 minute, but the organic traffic engagement time was 1 min 30 secs. So, what about their engagement rate? Of site visitors, 82.3 percent were engaged or 9,835 people out of 11,950. This key difference shows search engines, namely

Google, that the website has value to new users. It also means we were on the right track for content and copy on the website. The other key factor to verify our results were sessions versus engaged sessions. Users started 15,246 sessions. Out of these sessions 12,548 were engaged.

The scope of work included: creating meta descriptions for all pages and products, increasing website accessibility, updating the content flow, expanding on the website copy, refining each page, and creating product categories. Meta descriptions are the page description you see on a search results page. A perfect description is under 160 characters, describes that specific page, and is clear and concise.

Below is the data for 2021, 2022, and 2023.

Metric	2021	2022	2023
All Traffic	7,062	11,950	15,000
Organic Traffic	2,250	4,567	9,300
Organic Engaged Sessions	662	12,548	10,776
Organic Engagement Time	1 min. 30 sec.	52 seconds	1 min. 30 sec.
Retention Rate	9.5%	10%	15%

What the numbers tell us: In 2022 the work on the website combined with a marketing strategy involving social media and a few ads helped to build user growth by 355 visitors a month. The wording and ideal client focus that was generated for the website also worked for social media and ads. One consistent voice across the platforms. The downside is this company sells high ticket customizable products that can be returned. Even with multiple sales a week there was a high number of returns.

In 2023, the site had 15,000 visitors to the website. 92 percent of users were engaged or 14,720 people were engaged for 1 min 30 seconds, on average. Out of 15,000 people, 4,500 were new users. Parameter minimum for retention is 10 percent or 450. They retained 562 of the new users.

What the numbers tell us about consistency and staying focused on human behavior on websites is, it is a long game. Compare the numbers of 2021 with 7,100 users to 2023 where they had 16,000 users. That equates to 1300 visitors a month vs 592 in 2021.

CASE STUDY 3: Tomato Chip Company

After working with the Tomato Chip Company we were able to achieve great results in a short amount of time to help this brand reach Hidden Consumers.

My team and I only worked with this company from mid-July to the end of September. In the first 6 weeks we were able to connect the search term "tomato chips" to them and increase their organic search results. They had only been found by name, instead of a suggested item for Hidden Consumers, prior to that. We also discovered three Hidden Consumer bases for them. Their ideal client was primarily the person who wanted a healthier snack without additives or chemicals. My employee discovered one Hidden Consumer group that actively eats tomato chips, which helped us to increase the keyword connection faster. We had no numbers for the website to use for comparisons when we started.

I connected their website to Google Analytics 4 in July and data started coming in on July 30th.

Between July 30th and September 27th, they had:

- 191 users with a 45.67 percent engagement rate for 39 seconds.
- Their organic search traffic was 63 of the 191 users.
- Of the 63 people, 67 percent had engaged for 1 min and 5 secs.
- Retention was also good. Out of the 191 users 189 were new users.
- The minimum parameter for retention is 10 percent or in this case 19 people. They retained 47 new users. This means the work we did puts them on the right track to bring in their ideal client.

Metric	Organic	All Traffic
Traffic Engagement Rate Engagement Time	63 users 67% engaged (42 users) 1 min. 5 sec.	191 users 45.67% engaged 39 seconds
Retention		47 users

What the numbers tell us is that by focusing on their product we were able to quickly bring in their ideal client and a Hidden Consumer base. This helped to elevate their numbers. Our work focused on the ideal client, which also helped search engines to quickly identify who would want to see this product and find value in the website.

CASE STUDY 4: Traditional SEO versus Attract, Engage, and Convert

A client hired us to update some backend work on their website. They had hired a company to set up traditional SEO. Their website did a great job of bringing people to the site but minimal engagement from the users.

We updated the phrasing on page, the call-to-action buttons, and other basic backend work. We immediately saw the change in engagement.

Metric	Traditional SEO	Attract, Engage, and Convert	% Change
All Traffic	6,000	6,000	0%
All Traffic Engagement Rate	15% (900 users)	40% (2,400 users)	173% increase
Organic Traffic	4,000	2,400	40% decrease
Organic Engagement Time	16% (640 users)	60% (1440 users)	275% increase

What the data tells us is by creating an engaging website, we increased their ability to sell. The decrease in organic traffic does not bother me. Since the engagement rate of the organic traffic increased, the Signature

System engaged more organic traffic with the site at a higher volume than the traditional SEO was able to achieve. This is a fantastic example of why the work must focus on the end user. You can bring the world to your website and still have no sales.

A client of mine shared a great example. They had a client who over the last few years could no longer depend on traditional SEO to bring in clients. They had grown their business with no networking and strictly using SEO tactics. The company they worked for no longer brought in the clients they needed. So, the client switched to another SEO company only to achieve worse results. The client went back to the original SEO firm and still did not achieve what they needed .

Why did this happen? The problem came when Google made the transition to end-user focused SEO. All businesses have seen an increase in cold emails or LinkedIn messages from companies claiming to build links and get you found on search engines. If their processes were still working, you would not be receiving a cold outreach from them. Don't do link building to bring in traffic. Ensure the end user engages with your site, and you'll reach your Hidden Consumers.

GETTING QUALIFIED VISITORS

In the above case studies, you can see some of the data I looked at to measure success. It's not just about how many users came to the website. It's about the experience they had and if it converted. In traditional SEO, the focus is on drawing as many unqualified users to the website as possible. This leads to a lack of engagement on your site. Now with search engines placing emphasis on engagement and actions taken on full sites and individual pages, the result is lower organic traffic numbers. These lower numbers still consist of unqualified users, which means your website is taking up space without a purpose. It's not even selling you to new people who were told to check out your products.

A someone who helps companies market to Hidden Consumers, I know that a different approach is necessary for success. Your website is the foundation of a profitable marketing strategy. This is why data is so integral in reaching your customers. Your website must be set up to passively sell you or your product. And it all starts with good copy.

The content and copywriting problem usually starts with whoever built the website. Most companies use a website designer. This means your website will be aesthetically pleasing but no one but you will actually see it. When we work on the content and copy, we focus on your ideal client. We have a template we use for basic flow of the homepage to entice engagement with a call-to-action strategy that draws people into the website. Once the homepage flow is created, we can see the rest of the website flow coming into focus, identifying what pages are needed and what information needs to be on each page to help engage the user.

Once live, we will compare the CTA strategy to the data. Did the users behave predictably? Did they do something different? Does it make sense to alter the CTA strategy to what the users were looking for? Did the engagement time page match the expectation and parameter created? Was the overall website engagement time above the parameter? Did you meet Google's minimum parameter of 30 seconds? Or my parameter of a minimum of 1 minute?

The value of being curious cannot be understated. Part of my job is to always ask questions of my clients and of the data. I question my results to determine whether we are on the right track for each client.

In the world of Hidden Consumer marketing, your end user is your ideal client. As a brand, your goal should be to bring your ideal client to your site, not the world to your site. There is an old marketing adage that says, "If you market to everyone, you sell to no one." This is true for your website as well. The focus for your website needs to be on who you want to sell to or work with. Your call-to-actions must make sense to the user, your nav menu needs to be streamlined for easy use, and the organization of the pages needs to be logical.

What you shouldn't do is game the system. Don't overload your site with backlinks or fake out the algorithms. These steps might make you successful for a day or a month, but they won't lead to long-term success. The other problem with these practices is they don't focus on the end user. If you are looking to drive bots to your site, go for it. But your ideal client? Not so much.

We have not always achieved these results with all of our clients. For those who struggle with change, our system will test your limits of what you believe should be a "good website." We don't work with people who only want us to be glorified checklist completers. We have had clients who decided they wanted to stick to what they knew about websites and not let us do our job. These clients saw a downturn in numbers. They were not focused on who they wanted to work with. The goal was that the business owner had to like the website, and it had to be "pretty." Functionality for the user was not necessary in their world. If their thoughts around the website had worked, they would not have sought us out. I empathize with how hard change can be; but you cannot expect different results by doing the same things.

Today, we are more selective about who we work with when it comes to reaching Hidden Consumers. As a company focused on numbers and achieving results for our clients, change must happen. Some of the strategies we recommend can be thought-provoking and stress-inducing if you are not ready for change. And for the Hidden Consumer market, that application goes beyond food-related brands.

Beyond The Food And Beverage Industry

I CHOOSE TO WORK with the food and beverage industry primarily, but many areas can also use these techniques. I struggled with choosing between beauty and skin care, products, hotels, governments, and so much more. I found that the food and beverage industry, with an emphasis on natural and organic ingredients, was where Hidden Consumers Consulting could make the biggest impact. We could make grocery shopping safe for *everyone*. So how can what we do impact other industries? Here's a breakdown of what to consider and how to make your space marketable to Hidden Consumers if you are a non-food brand.

BEAUTY AND SKIN CARE

The number of people with various intolerances and allergies to ingredients is palpable. What companies do not realize is this does not only impact food. The products we use on or in our bodies can also be a source of reaction if they are not careful.

For example, people are having an increased reaction to Balsam of Peru, which is also a key ingredient from shampoos to cosmetics. When I chat with people in these groups, we try and exchange possible alternative products to use. Finding products that clearly state the ingredients isn't always easy, though. Like so many ingredients in food and cosmetics, most are hidden.

I'm using my own corn sensitivity as an example here, but the exercise of assessing ingredient lists in any of these products is useful no matter what a Hidden Consumer's allergies might be. The struggle comes from not knowing all the ingredients or not finding a product that does not contain the offending ingredients. Here is a list of beauty and skincare products the corn-sensitive Hidden Consumer struggles to buy:

- **Hand soap:** One of the most difficult products for me to find is soap not made from corn or derived from corn. In many cases, one-quarter of soap's ingredients are corn-based, including corn oil and products made from bioprocessing. As I discussed earlier in the book, Xanthan gum thickens and stabilizes soap, as well as food. You can also find it in hair gels and toothpaste. I currently have a safe soap made from goat's milk and olive oil, and they are the only ingredients.

- **Hair care products:** Corn syrup helps hair care products retain moisture. Citric acid is used to control pH balance. Cornstarch in dry shampoos binds with natural oils and reduces grease.[27] I had to stop using hair dryers and curling irons because of the damage they do to my hair. I have no products I can use to combat the damage. It's always a fun experience going to the salon now. The stylist always comments on how healthy my hair is and then asks what I use which is shampoo and conditioner and occasionally hair gel by the same company when I am dressing up for an event. All these products are unscented as well. I have in recent years found a somewhat safe hairspray, but I need to wash it out within 12 hours, or my scalp starts to turn red.

- **Toothpaste and floss:** I have a safe toothpaste I ordered from a company in Las Vegas. Floss is hard to find without the corn wax coating on it. They do have the issue of breaking faster, but I don't have to deal with the oral allergic reaction. Prior to fully understanding the severity of my allergy, my dentist was concerned about the health of my gums. We were seriously discussing dentures because it looked that bad. My tooth and gum sensitivity were so high that my gums seemed to bleed by just looking at them. Once I discovered toothpaste was the culprit everything changed. I bring my own toothpaste and floss to my dental visits now. My gums do not bleed like they used to unless my flossing is not up to par.

- **Perfumes, scented moisturizers, and body products** in general are the bane of my existence. Corn is often used as the base for alcohol used to carry the scent in the product. Corn-derivative ingredients may also be used to enhance texture or viscosity.

- **Cosmetics:** Cornstarch is found in body powders, skin care, lipsticks, eye, and facial makeup. Corn oil can be found in skin care products. Xanthan gum is a makeup stabilizer and thickener. I mentioned earlier in the book there is a large amount of corn in cosmetics without adequate regulations in the industry. I stopped wearing makeup for 6 years. I found safe mineral makeup I could wear that was only foundation, highlighter, and setting powder. But I had no color, like eye shadows or blush. It wasn't until a year or two before we moved to California that I finally found a company that sold everything from liner to lipstick. I even have a water-based nail polish I can occasionally wear as long as I remove it within 48 hours, which is not a big deal since water-based polish doesn't have longevity on your nails.

- **Facial cleansers** are another troubling area for Hidden Consumers to find something safe. I eventually found a company through the Corn Allergy Girl Community, Badger Balm. I was able to use their products up until 2018 or so. They made a change to their formula and packaging that I had reactions to and had to quickly find replacements.

- **Deodorant:** Cornstarch has an absorbent nature, which makes it a common ingredient in many hygiene items, including deodorants. It is also extremely uncomfortable to have a rash and hives on your underarm. I had to switch to a brand called Crystal. It's basically rock salt used as deodorant. It surprisingly works. This type of product made me wonder how much corn-based products force us into a cycle of needing corn-based products. I used to have a strong body odor. I could never find a perfect deodorant. But once I eliminated corn, my stench went away. I use less deodorant today than I did when using corn-based products and eating corn-based processed foods.

- **Diapers:** Cornstarch-based materials provide a super-absorbent core for diapers, while PLA, made from corn bioprocessing, can replace petroleum plastics and outer covers. Even baby powder is not safe. It is made from cornstarch.
- **Feminine hygiene products** also use corn. But you don't only find it in pads, you also find it in tampons. Besides the use of corn, you also find corn-derived materials. Synthetic ingredients, like rayon, are used in Tampax tampons. From the Tampax website in 2022, they stated rayon was used for the fiber of the tampon for its ability to absorb fluid and expansion ability to stop leaks.

Like food ingredients, you cannot trust a manufacturer to always use the same source to make a lab ingredient. Rayon, like nylon, can be made from corn. It is common for a manufacturer to use whatever ingredients they can get their hands on versus always using the same core ingredients. Do I know if Tampax does this? I don't. What I can tell you is I have reacted to every major brand of tampons. I cannot just go out and buy my feminine products at Target or any store within a 10-minute drive from my home. I must look for brands that are pure cotton with no additional fibers added.

One of the skin care companies I buy from made a change based on my recommendation. I first met the founder and bought a few trial-size products when visiting Sacramento in April 2024. I was concerned with the number of vitamins used in their products and asked about their source. The founder told me that all the natural ingredients used were selected because they were naturally high in vitamins, not due to additives. I recommended she note that on the ingredients section for each product it impacted. As a Hidden Consumer this distinction is critical. Had I not asked, I would have assumed the vitamins were additives, thus, being made from my allergen and not something I could buy. Simply explaining that it is naturally occurring in certain ingredients shows it is safe to buy without further research. The end result is a Hidden Consumer can now buy that product when they see it.

HOSPITALS, CLINICS, DENTAL OFFICES, AND VET OFFICES

From cleaning supplies to medications, hospitals and clinics are such an allergy producer for me, that I avoid going into the doctor's office at all costs. For the Hidden Consumer visiting any medical office, or even vet offices, can be a risk to our health. This area can also benefit from the Signature System by clearly stating they understand the needs of the Hidden Consumer.

Hospitals and Clinics

On the rare occasion I take the risk to go to a clinic, just by walking into the building I start to become lightheaded. My ability to think slows down. Some of the immediate issues that elicit an allergic response are the products used to clean the building. If the building is newer, I may also react to the carpet in the waiting area as well as the basic construction issues. Once in the exam room, I must be cautious about blood draws. Alcohol-based wipes used to sanitize the skin are made from ethyl-alcohol. I have developed a rash from the wipe which led to a rash and hives on my arm because of the alcohol getting into the tiny opening in my arm.

I don't have a latex allergy, but cornstarch is used in gloves. Even non-latex gloves are coated in cornstarch. Other issues involving cornstarch are surgical dressings. Cornstarch has super-absorbent properties which can help accelerate healing and reduce scarring in patients.

Another big issue related to hospitals and clinics is medication.

There are so many hidden ingredients in our meds. The lucky few who can have their meds compounded still have a chance to be treated by medical professionals. In my case, I have been turned away from medical care because my body cannot tolerate meds. Even before I knew of my corn intolerance and allergy, I struggled with medications being effective. I was diagnosed with migraines at the age of 2. In my late twenties, I went to a neurologist and asked for help. My headaches and migraine pain had become so severe it was interfering with my ability to work. I already had a known allergy to Imitrex which meant nothing in that family could be prescribed. All other medications had failed. I asked to know the cause of my atypical migraines and what my other options for treatment were. "None" was the response. Medication was the option for migraines; no other treatments existed. He then proceeded to tell me, since I was refusing all medications as treatment, he would no longer see me.

As my intolerances and allergies developed, this has become a much larger issue. I cannot safely be vaccinated; I cannot take any medications, and medical staff are unaware to the hidden dangers around allergies to medications. Most in the medical field don't even realize the extent of corn starch used in medications.

The key here is medical offices need to first be educated on potential allergies. The fact that the government does not recognize it as an allergen does not mean it does not exist. The second step is to listen to the patient with an open mind and not from their limited experience. I will say, as more and more people are developing intolerances and allergies the more nurses are becoming compassionate and understanding of the situation.

Dental Offices

In February of 2022, I had to have my first major oral procedure since discovering the corn allergy. I had to have a crown put on a tooth. Zein is the principal protein in corn and is extracted from corn gluten meal. It can be spun into fibers and biological scaffolding. It is then used to help repair damage in and around teeth. Thankfully, my dentist did not use a product that seemed to be this high in corn. However, back in 2012, I had a filling redone. I had tooth pain from that filling for roughly 5 years.

This is another area where understanding the depths of hidden ingredients is important. I have to fight through my bi-annual dental visits.

Until 2024, I did not have a dentist or hygienist that believed corn could be an issue. People who deal with wheat and gluten deal with the same disbelief. If I used the office's toothpaste and floss, I end up with a mouth full of blisters and sensitive gums for up to 48 hours after the appointment. As it is, I get a blister wherever the plastic water suction tube touches the inside of my mouth. Understanding the extent ingredients are causing problems for oral health is important.

Vet Offices

In October 2022, my cat, Empress Sheba de Meow Meow, had a dental cleaning done. This led to her vet finding an infected tooth eating away at her jawbone. We had the tooth removed. A few days later she developed an ulcer in her right eye. This required us to give her liquid gabapentin. Have you ever given liquid meds to a cat? This process requires one person to hold all paws and head still so the second person can use a syringe and force the meds into the side of the mouth. I held Sheba and my husband did the injection of the meds. Every time, I end up with some of the medicine on my right hand. Every time I would end up with a rash and hives if I did not rinse off my hand immediately.

Medication Implications

Pharmaceuticals or medications use cornstarch as a key ingredient in cellulose acetate phthalate (CAP). This ingredient coats pills to ensure their structural integrity, ease of swallowing, and timed release of medicine inside. It's also in intravenous solutions. Patients with low blood sugar are often given IV drips which contain dextrose, a corn derivative. I mentioned Band-Aids before, but dissolvable stents and structures are not even free of corn. Polylactic acid (PLA) stents and sutures dissolve away naturally after surgery. PLA is made from bioprocessed cornstarch. Then there are antibiotics. Microorganisms that create antibodies are often fed corn-based glucose in the lab. Corn is responsible for more than 85 antibiotics, including penicillin. Ironically, many people are resistant to penicillin.[28]

Due to the unique size, shape, and structure of the corn protein zein at the nanoparticle level, scientists in biomedical nanotechnology are even studying how it can deliver drugs that fight cancer. Which is amazing but horrifying to me at the same time because I may one day be allergic to such treatments.

These examples focus on my experience with corn, but others have similar experiences with different allergens like wheat or latex. The biggest issue in all these cases is the lack of knowledge from the medical team. From the day my allergist and allergy team agreed that corn was my issue to every medical encounter since then, doctors are either shocked or refuse to believe corn is an allergen. The other people who suffer from unrecognized intolerances and allergies share similar experiences. These reactions are harmful to the Hidden Consumer.

To be more inclusive, doctors need to understand they are not gods. They do not know all the medical information that exists in the world today, let alone all the information currently being studied and needing to be discovered. If a patient has been diagnosed by another professional, trust them. Unless the patient is in your office for a second opinion, it is not your job to deny their diagnosis.

HOTELS AND RESTAURANTS

More can be done to make the dining experience safer for those with intolerances and allergies anywhere food is served. Here are two examples from a hotel and restaurant.

When I travel, I bring my own food whenever possible. Even when flying to a destination, I need to ensure I can eat safely—otherwise what's the point of a vacation if I am sick the entire time?

If you are serving food, there are a few quick ways to improve consumer happiness (and not just for Hidden Consumers). Honestly, discuss all ingredients that go into a meal. If your sauce uses canned tomatoes, garlic, and spices, list all the ingredients. Let the consumer decide for themselves if a meal is safe for them.

If you hold events with buffets, create a card for each food container with what is used to make that product. One of the caterers I work with did not realize she used garlic in every item she made. Garlic is an intolerance for many and not listing it means people could suffer abdominal discomfort and not be comfortable using that caterer for their future events.

Why Eating Out is Risky

For many Hidden Consumers to eat out, they need to put precautions in place to keep themselves safe. Most understand you cannot depend on restaurants or their staff to understand each individual's level of sensitivity. Even today with all my precautions in place, I still get "corned." One area that is always a high risk for me is eating out at restaurants.

Before going somewhere new, I must look at the menu and see what they offer. Do they depend on sauces for every menu item? I look at pictures to see how food is plated. Plastic or ceramic? If it looks safe, I will try eating in the restaurant. I go as far as to carry my own silverware with me. Occasionally I will find a location that looks good, but they only have plastic silverware. Here's the key, I don't tell the staff I have a corn allergy. Here's an example of why.

In November 2022, I really wanted to be at an in-person event for an association chapter for which I was the marketing director. The program director chose the restaurant. We had a special menu to order from. Each person had their choice of appetizer and entrée, and everyone had the same dessert. I realized there was nothing on the entire menu I could eat.

The president of our chapter contacted the chef, and I was allowed to order from the regular menu. This is not a restaurant I would normally visit due to the heavy dependence on sauces for each option. I picked what looked like the safest option. However, the restaurant was informed that my issue was corn. I also had to clarify that I could not have the balsamic onions because vinegar is made from corn.

The night of the event was amazing to be around people in the chapter. The waitress in charge of our table let me know there was an issue with one of the side dishes having corn in it. I said I did not want rice or a side dish with the meal. No corn means no corn. When the meal arrived, I could tell something was off.

We wrapped up and I was home by 9 pm. I started to feel sick and went to bed at 30 minutes later. At 1:51 am a headache starting to take shape. I went through my ritual of drinking 18 oz of water, heating up my heat wrap, and plugging in my heating pad. I went back to bed and hoped this would knock it out. I woke up at 4 am with a full-blown migraine. At 7am, I had a meeting with my employee. I went through what I could to rest and take care of my head. Our meeting lasted 3 minutes. I became so nauseous I had to abruptly end the session. Thankfully, my bathroom is not far from my office.

Guess what made an appearance? Four kernels of corn. Was corn deliberately placed in my food? I don't know. What I can tell you is whenever I tell a restaurant I have a corn allergy, corn ends up in my food. Not a lot. Sometimes it's only one piece, this time it was four. One of the digestive issues I have had for as long as I can remember, is my stomach shutting down and not digesting food. This is typically what happens with a migraine. But when corn is added to the mix, it is taken to another level.

Migraines seem to slow the digestive process to almost a stop, but food only comes back up if corn is involved. The day after a migraine, I have to deal with diarrhea as my body cleans out the rest of my system.

The migraine passed 36 hours later. The next 24 hours I had to stay close to a bathroom. The effects of corn on my body however will not be over in 24 hours. I will still be dealing with bloating and discomfort for the next week. Corn is a toxin to my body.

The bigger problem is the mindset of those without allergies. These people seem to think they have a right to test my body's response. If I don't react in the restaurant, they think they are vindicated in not following instructions. I ended up losing a day of work. I own my business and losing a day of work is not acceptable.

Now think of the people you know who have issues with food. What you see versus what they go through are two different experiences. Most of us with food issues hide the full experience from others.

If you are a hotel or restaurant owner and are doing well enough to not need additional customers, then you are not concerned with this. But if you are struggling, then how you approach those with food sensitivities could make a difference. A restaurant or a hotel cannot accommodate every issue that exists, but if you change the staff's mindset on being open to listening, you have started in the right direction.

The next step is to be clear with all staff members about what is in each recipe. You don't need to give out the family secrets, but the staff need to be able to answer questions for those trying to stay safe and give you money.

PROCESSING, PRESERVING, AND PACKAGING

Today I use my knowledge to help companies in the specialty food and beverage industries understand how to better communicate with their customers and Hidden Consumers. My focus on the food industry is currently on the business-to-consumer side. There are many subindustries within that can also impact the Hidden Consumer. We touched on a few areas like manufacturing and ingredient making industries already. Three areas involved with manufacturing and ingredients are Processing, Preserving, and Packaging industries. Processing focuses on the ingredients and how they are made. Preservatives are what gives a food or product shelf life. Packaging is exactly how it sounds; it is what the product is wrapped or boxed in. The Hidden Consumer needs to avoid these three key areas where added ingredients and materials are used.

Preservatives

Preservatives have become a buzzword, similar to gluten-free. In both situations, these buzzwords have caused real harm to those who need to be careful. Companies do not understand the chemical compounds they are using to help you keep your food longer. For the average person, this is becoming a big deal. The ingredients used for preserving food and other products are linked to health risks like chronic pain, kidney failure, and more. But if you are marketing to a growing community of Hidden Consumers, you need to know what ingredients are being used to preserve your products to accurately answer any of their questions.

In addition to being used to prolong the lifespan of foods, preservatives are also used in medicine to prevent microbial contamination. You can find it mostly in acetaminophen, insulin, and cough syrup. In cosmetics and personal care products they help to prevent the growth of harmful bacteria.

According to the American Chemistry Council, the FDA regulates preservatives. I tend to question anything that states "regulated by the FDA or USDA." People who have corn allergies are not recognized by the FDA or the USDA and are not considered in their regulations. Those of us with a corn allergy must be more aware and educated on what we eat and use for products. According to the American Chemistry Council, "Preservatives in medicines and drugs are generally considered to be 'inactive ingredients' by the FDA. Its Inactive Ingredients Database provides information on inactive ingredients in FDA-approved drug products."

It's important to know the difference between inactive ingredients and active ingredients. Active ingredients are those that provide medicinal benefits. Inactive ingredients are used for the delivery of the active ingredients. Cornstarch itself is not used as an ingredient for medical benefit. It is, however, used to help bind the ingredients together. The patients ingest it but not for a pharmaco-logical purpose.

Preservatives are generally derived from corn and other ingredients including corn derivatives themselves. However, they can be made from many different sources. This is why this industry needs to be more transparent with how they make ingredients in order to keep all consumers safe. For example, preservatives are described as being made from natural chemicals such as salt or alcohol. In the United States, I have found that all alcohol-based preservatives are derived from corn. But it is common for synthetic or man-made chemicals to also be used for the purpose for creating a preservative. Artificial preservatives like sodium nitrate, sodium benzoate, and propionate are typically used in food preparation.

In this situation, you must put two-and-two together. Sodium nitrate, sodium benzoate and propionate are all mostly derived from corn. It is also important to know food and products have different sets of regulations. Cosmetics have preservatives as well. The difference is the preservatives in cosmetics do not need FDA premarket approval and they monitor product recalls.

Cosmetics were something I had to originally give up, same with hair products. I finally found two safe brands. What you need to look for are companies who are trying to be ethical in procuring their ingredients. My favorite cosmetics company, Honeybee Gardens, is vegan and has multiple certifications. Not all their products are safe for me. I still must read labels and determine if my body will tolerate an ingredient.

Packaging

I don't know if I can fully state how disappointed I was in finding packaging to be an issue. There is a significant number of products that I thought were safe, but the packaging was the downfall. The issues ranged from the use of corn-based plastics to cornstarch coating to keep the product from sticking to canned and environmentally friendly bottles and packaging of products.

Canned

Even in canned products you find corn. The biggest issue I found is corn starch or corn-based plastics being used to coat the inside of the cans. This helps keep food from sticking to the inside. Around the same time I was going through this process, Ball canning jars started using cornstarch on the inside of their lids. No canning was going to be in my future.

When food is canned, the jar is heated up to create the seal. In turn, this heats up the cornstarch and contaminates the food within the jar. The number of Hidden Consumers that Ball lost in consistent sales would have made an impact. In my various health and allergy communities, this was a major blow to many who could garden safely. They no longer had a way to store food.

In all other aspects, canned food should be safe. Preservatives are not used or needed in the process. The canning process involves a high-temperature heat which destroys microorganisms and inactivates enzymes to keep food safe. So why is canning so unsafe, not just for those with corn allergies, but for all children and adults? The BPA lining in canned goods is linked to toxicity in humans, especially children.

Prior to 2008 BPA was extensively used in bottling and packaging, studies came out showing how toxic it was to human health. In true FDA fashion, they ignored or downplayed the toxicity of BPA. It was up to retailers and states to put pressure on the industry to change its practices and remove BPA. In 2009 20 states passed legislation to reduce exposure of BPA to kids. By 2010 the FDA decided to "express concern" over the use of BPA in canned products. But as of today, BPA is still legal to use in canned products in most states. The FDA has not banned its use like other countries have done.

The other issue is cross-contamination. From cleaning supplies to canned food products, you can't be certain any store product is safe. Everything I buy is a gamble on my safety at various levels. Like many Hidden Consumers, I chose to cut canned foods out to eliminate one more area to have to be concerned about.

Plastics

Most plastics, as of today, seem to be made from corn. The amount of corn used to make the plastic varies. The FDA has an entire page dedicated to the topic of food packaging that comes in contact with food.

The FDA states that, "A food contact substance is a substance that comes into contact with food and is not intended to have a technical effect in such food. This includes food packaging and its components, processing equipment, food preparation surfaces, or cookware. Other examples include substances that are added to or applied on packaging surfaces, such as adhesives, colorants, certain uses of antimicrobials, and antioxidants. Certain food contact substances are considered indirect food additives."[29]

Even though packaging is not intended to be consumed, the reality is it is degrading with your food in it. The current research is pointing to a connection between microplastics and colorectal cancer. I am a self-proclaimed wine snob, completely because of the corn issues in wine. But boxed wine has never been something I wanted to drink. If we look at how boxed wine, or even your bottled water, are kept in plastics, you go to take a drink and without realizing it you are ingesting microplastics with your beverage. Plastic is being found in human stomachs in small quantities.

The main issue here is the environment. The Hidden Consumer concerned about the environment might want to look for items not made of plastic in order to protect the world where they live.

Paper Products and Other Types of Packaging

Facial tissue, toilet paper, and even paper towels are made from corn. Even the cardboard tube we used to play with as kids uses glue from dextrin. To avoid corn, you have to know what to look for. The facial tissue I can use has no scents and no lotions. Both scents and lotions are based on corn derivatives. I also buy generic brands. Toilet paper can be harder to find. I went through at least five brands before finding one that worked for me.

You can also find corn in business cards, stationery, envelopes, notepads, basically anything ordered from a printing service, including the ink used to print on the product. Different inks require different "body." In Newspapers ink needs to be soft and fluid, while others are thick and stiff. Cornstarch is added to control the consistency of each ink. Does this mean I don't use these products? No. But I do have to be aware of it for my safety. Prolonged exposure will make me break out from touching corn-based inks or paper products.

Remember Styrofoam? It is being replaced by biodegradable products made from bioprocessing cornstarch. Check your paper and plastic cups. They may say "made from corn" right on them. Again, it's probably helpful to the environment but maybe we should look at other alternatives instead of overplanting corn.

Why Environmentally Friendly Packaging is Dangerous

We've all seen the images on the news or in our social media feeds showing mass amounts of plastics floating in the oceans. We have heard how cruise ships and other ocean-going vessels dump their waste directly into the water.

It turns out when a product is touted as being environmentally friendly, it generally has corn in it. Corn is a naturally occurring material. This makes it an ideal candidate for use in products to help with decomposition. However, for the growing number of people with corn allergies this is one more area we have to look out for to keep ourselves healthy.

Here is a list of the ways your Hidden Consumers will find corn in environmentally-friendly, and non-friendly, packaging:

1. BPA-free linings are made from acrylic, polyester, non-BPA epoxies, polyvinyl chloride (PVC) copolymers, or olefin polymers. Food grade linings and packaging almost always use corn in some form in everything from the extraction process of elements to creating the packaging that encases our food.
2. Green compostable packaging is created from natural materials that will decompose back into the earth. These materials are typically made from plants like corn.
3. Slurry ice, small ice particles in liquid, is used in packaging frozen foods. The liquid can be sodium chloride, ethanol, ethylene glycol, and propylene glycol, all of which are derived from corn. It is used in air conditioning, packaging, industrial cooling processes, supermarkets, and the cooling and storage of

fish, produce, poultry, and other perishables.

4. Ethylene is naturally produced in corn. It is widely used in the chemical industry for food packaging, film, toys, food containers, bottles, pipes, antifreeze, carpets, insulation, and the list goes on and on and on.

5. Green cell foam is made from corn. It is also certified for backyard composting and industrial facilities. You can also disintegrate it in water.

6. PLAs, or polylactic acid, are made from corn or cane sugar. Mostly are made from corn sugar to reduce the price.

In my own journey, some of the harder lessons were around food packaging and corn contamination. I have allergic reactions to drinking water out of plastic bottles. Why? Plastics for food are generally food-grade and are made from corn. When I leave my house or travel, I need to take my own safe bottles of water with me. Or I must know where I can buy still water in glass bottles. Why do we have such a dependency on corn-based plastics? A belief that it is safer for the environment. I beg to differ on the topic.

Let's start by destroying a myth. Corn-based plastics do not solve our plastic pollution problem. One of the biggest benefits of corn-based plastics is its ability to break down faster when buried. But what you are not told is that in normal conditions it still takes 1,000 years for the plastic to decompose in a landfill. *The Scientific American* wrote an article discussing the pros and cons of corn-based plastics, also known as polylactic acid or PLAs.[30]

The top four points from the article were:

1. Corn-Based Plastics / PLA's biodegrade slowly. You need specific created recycling centers to biodegrade these types of plastics in 3 months.

2. There are limited number of industrial-grade composting facilities across the US In 2008, when the article was published there were 113. In 2025, there are 4700 according to the USDA.

3. PLA is generally made from genetically modified corn.

4. People need to separate their corn-based plastics / PLAs from their other recyclables.

This article was written in 2008, but we still have these issues. If you aren't willing to separate out your recycling now, are you going to be willing to separate your PLAs? I am going to say no. And for the record, I do separate my recycling from normal trash and my food waste is separated from trash and composted as well.

Next let's look at water from a plastic bottle, it is likely the bottle will be made from a PLA. How did I learn this? First, by getting sick after taking a sip of water from a plastic bottle. The industry wants you to believe that the materials to make the bottle won't leach into the product. They are wrong. After I became ill, I started researching how plastic bottles are made. Low and behold, corn sugar and cornstarch are the main ingredients in most plastic water bottles.

My choices for water are unfiltered (water filters are made from plastic) from my kitchen tap or specific glass-bottled waters. Mountain Valley sells water in a green bottle, and I react to their water. Is it the bottle? Or is the cross-contamination from the facility? As of 2024, I have been on the hunt for glass bottled water. Icelandic is the one I am finding most often. I am lucky to have fewer reactions from my kitchen tap water than other Hidden Consumers. Corn contamination due to agricultural runoff can make it difficult for many people with a corn allergy to drink tap water.

But it goes beyond bottles. In fact, most products packaged in plastic wrap are made from some level of corn. You will find the issue in Styrofoam as well with the soaker pad and other packaging I have already listed.

As I mentioned above, BPA liner is used in cans, including aluminum. This is where the BPA-Free lining comes into play. I did not know until recently the amount of corn used in the packaging of cans. You'll have to read my section on the FDA and BPA to find out why this is a much bigger issue than corn.

I avoid store bought food and beverages that are packaged in any type of can. I do use metal water bottles, usually double-walled, for my own water usage. The difference is I don't clean them with citric acid, and they are not lined in a corn-based plastic liner or BPA.

I remember going out for ice cream not long after the start of my corn journey. My husband and I chose a creamery with better ingredients to give me a chance at not reacting to the food. I ordered what looked like the safest option and ordered it in a cup. This required me to eat it with a plastic spoon. Two bites in and a wave of nausea swept over me, and the headache stepped in. I know now that the cup and spoon were the culprit. To-go cups are made from paper with a corn-based wax lining to keep the paper from deteriorating with food in it. The corn-based wax does leach into your food. This happens more when heated up, say like in a coffee to-go cup. The spoon, like most plastic tableware, is also made from PLAs.

I have discovered the hard way many companies use cornstarch coated packaging for their products. Therefore, I cannot trust buying anything in a grocery store. Do you have plastic bottles in your pantry or refrigerator that claim you will get every drop of the product out? Massive amounts of cornstarch are used to make that bottle. Did you buy a lovely "organic" chocolate bar? The packaging will be lined with cornstarch or wrapped in corn-based plastic.

Beyond the effect on our environment and food, there are a minimum of 500,000 people with some level of corn allergy. A minimum. That is just in the United States. Across the globe our citric acid, dextrose, and other corn-based ingredients are shipped to be the base ingredients for their food. Links are starting to show up in countries from Sweden to the United Kingdom to Mexico to some nations in Africa of the impact on the human body. Poor health, from diabetes to cardiac arrest, are side-effects of eating too much processed food. Not only are we consuming it directly, but indirectly through packaging.

The bonus my research has given me is a more environmentally friendly lifestyle. Plastics are not a major part of my life anymore. I use stainless steel water bottles with steel and bamboo tops. My leftovers are stored in glass containers. Most, unfortunately, have a plastic lid so I must be sure my food doesn't touch the lid or cover it with safe aluminum foil.

FARMER'S MARKETS

Farmers markets will vary from state to state. The regulations around what is a "farmer's market" may be weak, like in Minnesota or strong like in California. The public assumes that real farmers support all farmer's markets. The reality is quite different. Customers can help different farmer's markets promote how they determine which farmers to let in.

In some cases, farmer's markets are just glorified markets with no actual farmers vending at the event.

I realized early on how the "organic" produce grown for grocery stores still made me sick. At the time, we were living in a suburb of Minneapolis. For people who don't live in the Midwest, farming is limited due to the seasons. If you are lucky you can plant in March or April but typically May through October is the time to plant, grow, and harvest. Once the snow hits, nothing can happen but planning for the next season. This means in the winter months the only vegetables I would have would be root vegetables that would keep over the winter, like potatoes, squash, and beets.

My allergy very much created a situation where I had to eat and store food similar to my great-great grandparents. I could not use canning jars for my food, so I had to survive mostly on potatoes and beets for a minimum of 6 months out of the year. Modern homes are not exactly built for this type of lifestyle, especially the inside units of townhomes.

In my intolerance and allergy world, that meant I needed to find a farmer's market to buy food. But not all farmer's markets are created equally. When I lived outside Minneapolis, I had two choices, the Saint Paul Farmer's Market or the Minneapolis Farmer's Market. Everything I had learned about how corn is hidden led me to read the vendor applications for each farmers market. I wanted to know how safe the food was at each market before I tried it. I was looking for was any clue that told me what level of organic food I could find.

Here are highlights from the application to be a vendor for Saint Paul's Farmer's Market:

Saint Paul Farmer's Market only allows producers who are members of the Saint Paul Growers Association, Inc. This means only people who grow their own produce, raise the animals, or make the cheese can sell to the public at the St. Paul Farmers Market. As a consumer this gives me confidence in the safety of the product I am buying from their location.

The other major highlight is each vendor must submit regular inspections, including surprise visits. Again, as a consumer, this knowledge shows me the market, and the farmers are dedicated to ensuring authenticity of what is being sold and who is vending the product.

Reading the requirements for application helped solidify the market's mission of being a true farmer's market. The product and produce sold at the Saint Paul market had to be verifiable from the farmer's land. The Saint Paul market clearly wanted to set themselves apart from their competition.

I then investigated the Minneapolis Farmers Market. Here are the highlights from the vendor application:

"Vendor Application is no longer available online."

In the early days of determining where to find safe food, Minneapolis Farmer's Market had their vendor requirements online. Iin the last decade, they updated their website, which looks great, and removed their vendor application. Per their website:

"Our market vendors' attendance and stall assignments vary on a daily basis and depend on the seasonality of their products. We host vendors that have a legacy of over 5 generations of farming and also allow space for new businesses to get their start at our market. Browse our list of vendors below to learn more. Interested in becoming a vendor? We are currently accepting applications for local growers. If you want more information, please visit the market office during operational hours and ask for a manager."

As a person with food allergies and intolerances, I found this suspicious. Why would you hide key information about how vendors are allowed to bring items to sell? After seeing what St. Paul publicly requested of their farmers, this came across as deliberately trying to hide information. I did reach out via their contact form on the website to see if they would share any information with me. I did not receive a response.

Why did I take the extra step? Because the Minneapolis Farmers Market is known for allowing vendors to buy from Bix Produce and have the food delivered before the market opens. This means you do not know which stall has food grown by the farmer for the market or the same vegetables you buy at the grocery store.

After this work, I obviously chose the Saint Paul Farmer's Market as my safest choice for food year-round. Today, I would make the same decision based on what I found online and the lack of response from the Minneapolis Farmers Market.

The Hidden Consumer must go the extra mile to deep dive into almost all aspects of the world around us because of the lack of transparency. The public's knowledge and distrust of grocery stores, farmers markets, and food in general is well founded.

The number of people who are getting sick from eating outweighs those who have no reactions. To stay safe, people are asking questions and being denied answers. This makes the vendor, company, or market look untrustworthy. The keys to marketing are know, like, and trust. Without trust, you don't have sales.

What I can tell you from having shopped at the farmer's market since 2018 is simply not all the farmers are safe to shop with. I shop at a certified farmers' market every Saturday, but through trial and error I have found vendors I can safely buy food from. What I eventually discovered, which led to a new list of questions for certified farmers, was some farmers do not rinse with water. They rinse dirt off their produce with soap or anti-bacterial products. Since anti-bacterial products are made with corn-based alcohol, and soaps are made from other corn derivatives, I react.

But when I find the right farmer to buy from it's like being back in my grandpa's garden and pulling peas right off the vine or picking lettuce. The vegetables may still have traces of soil or there may be a bug that's the size of your pinky nail. But the taste is perfect.

GOVERNMENTS AND CITIES

Governments are supposed to be for the people, but unfortunately, they work hard to exclude people from participating in events. This includes accessibility as much as letting people eat and drink water safely.

Accessibility

Have you ever attended a local event hosted by your city? I had to stop because the city refuses to be accessible. The next time you go to an outdoor event look to see if they have removed the handicap parking to put up tents.

Every outdoor event in my city from the farmer's market to community celebrations sets up **on** the handicap parking spots. I did complain and instead of keeping the events free, they started charging disabled people to attend. The fee was to bus disabled people in, and able-bodied people could still attend for free. The solution could have been to not use the handicap spots. Instead, they chose to deter disabled people from being at any community event.

Beyond physical access, accessibility should also be considered for those with visual and hearing issues. Color contrasts on banners, microphone for those speaking, and if using screens, you should have closed captioning as well.

Events

When holding an event with food vendors the city or local government should be concerned about potential allergic threats to the citizens. There should be guidelines in place to discuss what food vendors will be present and at a minimum what food may pose potential allergic risk. A quick statement on the web page about the event could state: "There will be a vendor on site cooking peanuts." Give people the option to prepare themselves for the event. I can be in an outdoor environment with corn being popped, I just cannot stay long in the vicinity. If I smell popcorn, I double-time it out of the area. But I know it will be present, and I always keep myself aware of my surroundings.

GAS STATIONS

Gas Stations and highways may not be as obvious areas for those wanting to bring in the Hidden Consumer. Consideration of contaminants at the gas pump could make Hidden Consumers safer and feel more welcome. Clear disclosure of healthier food and beverage options within gas stations could help Hidden Consumers find the products they need. As it is now, I have had some extreme situations with highways and gas stations.

Minnesota life was filled with corn-contamination. Ethanol, a corn-based gas, is sold in the United States. The most common blend of gasoline and ethanol is E10 where the mixture is 10 percent ethanol and 90 percent gasoline. In Minnesota you can buy E85 or flex fuel.

E85 is a high-level ethanol-gasoline blend containing 51 to 83 percent ethanol. The pro is it is cheaper than gasoline. The con is it costs more per mile because it has less energy per volume. The reduced energy leads to a 15 to 27 percent fewer miles driven.

I have reactions to airborne corn. Ethanol makes me sick. In the early days of my corn allergy, I used E85 in my vehicle. I would get a headache at the gas station and not connect it to the gasoline. I would then get sick every time I drove my vehicle due to the fumes in the car. But other issues also developed. I would be driving down the road, interstate, or highway and someone would be next to me in traffic, and I would get sick. It does not happen as often in California as it did in Minnesota.

DEALERSHIPS AND MOVIE THEATERS

There are hidden allergens in both car dealerships and movie theaters. Both pop fresh popcorn inside which limits your Hidden Consumers with airborne corn allergies from using your services or watching movies on the big screen.

Did you know cornstarch hardens when heated? This protects spark plugs from the high temperatures and acid solvents in car engines. Which is cool, right? I may get frustrated with how much cornstarch is used everywhere, but some of the innovations are amazing.

Another area you will find is in your tires. Once upon a time I worked in the commercial tire industry. I worked in a shop that repaired commercial tires as an administrative assistant. I could never figure out why I always reacted if I stepped into or was near an open door to the repair bays. I would always get nauseous. It turns out rubber is made from bioprocessed cornstarch. This reduces rolling resistance and weight for better fuel economy and better traction. For long haulers, fuel economy is important. In Germany, researchers are even developing paint for cars that is derived from cornstarch. It will automatically repair minor scratches.

You cannot talk about corn when out in public and not talk about movie theaters. I had to immediately stop going to the movies. I cannot even tell you about the last movie I saw in a theater because it's been so long. The amount of popcorn in the building makes me sick just walking by an open door to the theater complex. Going into the building isn't ever going to happen. I know the first movie my husband went to without me was in 2015. The movie was the latest *Star Wars* trilogy, *The Force Awakens*. I was bummed about not being able to go to the movies with him. Even today, I would love to enjoy going to the movies, but I know the risk isn't worth it.

The point here is we take for granted how products and food in our lives are made. My reaction is to corn but other Hidden Consumers have other concerns based around their ingredients and materials sensitivities. The key for each industry is to be aware that different people have different reactions to the same ingredients.

AIRPORTS AND TRAVEL

The biggest issue with traveling for most Hidden Consumers is air travel. Concerns range from plastic filters in all water fountains to restrictions on being able to keep yourself safe to restrictions on what you can travel with for food and drink. As an extreme example, the TSA usually asks me to go without food and drink because what is safe for me doesn't fit their needs.

No two airports have the same training or policies regarding "medical necessity." For example, Lee and I used to like to travel. As I was determining what was safe to eat and how to cook my food safely, we put traveling on hold. As I figured out what I would need to keep myself safe and headache / migraine free we started looking into travel again.

Our first big trip was in 2016 to Arizona for Chicago Cubs Spring Training. We found an Airbnb that had all stainless-steel pots and pans. The cooking utensils were not plastic or silicone. They also had ceramic plates and non-plastic glasses.

I knew I would need to look up regulations on bringing my safe water into the airport and onto the plane. I went as far as to get a letter from the doctor for medical necessity. The day we flew out of Minneapolis for Arizona came. We had to go to the airport early, in case of issues, but I did not expect the issue that ended up developing that morning.

During the security check, I explain I have water in my water bottle, and it is a medical necessity. I also explain that I have a doctor's note, as directed to do so by the TSA website. The TSA agent tells me he doesn't accept the note because it *could* be fake. My question is why does the TSA ask for it then? He said he was unaware that it was recommended. He then proceeds to tell me I am not allowed to have my safe water. He is going to dispose of it because it might be a bomb. I asked him to get me the manager. He was the manager. I ask if he can test the water or the bottle. If he doesn't allow me water, I will need to go without hydration until I reach my Airbnb which will not be for another 9 hours.

By this point, I am scared. Lee said I went "white as a ghost." He hadn't seen me lose that much color in my face and not be sick. I kept fighting for my safe water. The bottle alone would not be easy to replace, but to go without any water because he needed to go on a power trip? I continued to say my water was a medical necessity. Another agent finally stepped in and said we can easily test this. He took my water bottle and removed the cap. He placed the bottle in a machine and put a paper strip on top of it. Seconds later he says it's safe. I was allowed to take my water bottle and go to the gate.

I wish I could say this was an isolated incident. But I can't. Every single time I fly it is a similar situation. This past year, it happened all over again with a woman with gray hair. I said I needed my water bottle for medical necessity. She asked why. I explained I am allergic to plastic (it's easier than saying corn). She said it did not matter. All the water at the airport water fountains was safe because of the filters. I explained filters are made of plastic and I am allergic to them. She said it was not possible and proceeded to take my water bottle to dump out the contents. At this point, another agent stepped in and asked, "Did you tell her this was for a medical necessity?" I said "Yes." He tested the water bottle, gave it back to me, and sent me on my way. Every year it is the same issue. I have never had this issue in Phoenix, San Diego, Los Angeles, South Dakota, or San Francisco to name a few. I have run into quick moments of needing to repeat medical necessity, but nothing to the extent I have consistently gone through at MSP.

CLEANING PRODUCTS

Air fresheners from plugins to spray cans to carpet powders all can be rife with danger for the Hidden Consumer. For me, I have yet to find an air freshener that does not use ethyl alcohol for its base. To be clear, I stopped using all types of air fresheners a decade ago. Ethyl is corn derived, and I am airborne reactive to corn and its derivatives. Everything in the United States seems to start with corn-based alcohol. This includes cleaning supplies. An example of how sensitive I am to air fresheners still today happened while waiting to pick my husband up from work. I was sitting in my vehicle with the window down. A car pulled up and parked next to me and put both windows down. The wave of noxious fumes from her "air fresheners'" gave me an instant headache. I posted on Facebook that if you need that much moldy corn to get rid of the smell, maybe you should clean out your car. I really don't think the average person understands how scents affect those around them.

Between my disability and my allergy, it made cleaning some rooms of the house impossible. For example, the bathroom. Again, everything is corn based, and scents are corn based. Apparently, cleaning product manufacturers think we want our houses to smell like flowers or the ocean. Why can't we have unscented cleaning products? Is it because your product doesn't clean anything? Do you need the scent to hide your products' shortcomings? Even products that are not scented can still pose a problem due to the amount of synthetic ingredients created from corn. I have to choose items with minimal ingredients. They pass the test if I can be in the room while using the product and not get sick.

In your laundry detergent, cornstarch brightens fabric and removes dirt during the washing process. Citric acid, a corn and black mold product, is made through bioprocessing. It increases the cleaning power and helps soften water. However, this is not limited to your laundry detergent. You will also find it in your dishwashing detergent for the sink and dishwasher. The amount of corn-based ingredients in all types of dishwasher detergents and cleaning agents meant I had to stop using the dishwasher. I had to find safe dishwashing soap so I could hand wash my dishes again. This is a constant struggle. I am always trying a new product to see how it affects the skin on my hands or my reactions after eating a meal.

I used to love burning candles. I had a 1-gallon tote full of candles before this all began. The matches have cornstarch on the heads as a binder and to aid ignition. Paper matchsticks often include cornstarch to increase their rigidity. The candle itself is typically made from a corn-based wax or has a scent that uses corn in its ingredients.

CONSTRUCTION

Another issue I learned of early on in my journey was an ongoing debate on off-gassing of products. I can tell you from an allergy perspective, yes, many new products off-gas, especially in new homes. If a construction company uses alternative methods for construction, they could benefit by reaching out to the Hidden Consumer. Modern day construction practices are becoming harder for more and more people to tolerate. The Hidden Consumer could have issues with anything from walls, flooring types, paint on the wall to almost anything used to build a home.

A great example of off-gassing is when my husband and I were house shopping in 2020. We looked at brand-new homes, built and waiting for their first families to move in. I could not even walk through a new home. I would step in and be instantly sick with a headache, which can quickly turn into a migraine, nausea, rash and hives, and runny, itchy eyes. When people say they walk into a brand-new home and love the smell, I typically gag.

The other issue with newly built homes is drywall. The core of drywall is gypsum with layers of paper boards, thick cardboard, on top. These layers are all held together with an adhesive made from cornstarch.

Flooring

The Corn Refiners of America love telling you all the way corn is used in your home. Most of the information below comes from their website at corn.org.

Did you know carpet and tile are made from corn? I mean, let's celebrate using all the parts of corn and not throwing usable items into the trash. When you consider that so many products are corn dependent, it creates more waste than other products. So how do manufacturers get corn into our flooring options? Tiles can be made using biopolymer. This synthetic ingredient is made using natural resources. Corn being an inexpensive natural ingredient makes a good choice to keep costs down and profits high. In carpet, corn sugar can replace nylon, or companies can use corn-based nylons to make your carpet. The corn lobby pushes this by saying corn-based products are durable. But for someone with a corn allergy this is concerning to say the least.

A few years before we moved, we worked with A-1 Flooring out of Andover, Minnesota to replace our ancient carpet. Lee and I did the demo, and that's how I learned I would get really sick from carpet removal. Part of the problem was not only the carpet, but the scented carpet powder I had used overtime. It turns out I, like almost everyone, used too much and my vacuum could not pick up all the granules. There were areas of powder build-up under the carpet and on the subfloor.

The other issue with flooring is when glue is used. From the scent to the actual product, I can have multiple reactions. It doesn't matter if it is a glue stick, a hot glue gun, or even super glue I will have an allergic response. I am someone who likes crafting and creating this is troublesome when I have a project that requires glue. A project that should take minutes will take me hours, so I have time to walk away and remove myself from the scent and product. Now if this is on my floor, it becomes a much bigger issue. The amount of glue used, the strength of the glue or adhesive used will intensify the smell in my environment leaving me sick for an unspecified amount of time.

But carpet continues to be a source of allergies decades after they have been laid. Why? Because cleaning products are made from corn. Do you use a liquid carpet cleaner? Corn was used to make the cleaner. Use a powder carpet freshener to make your room smell "nice"? It's made from corn. Carpet, in my opinion, is also gross because it traps in dust and other allergens into your home. Carpet is literally an allergy attack waiting to happen.

Walls

After buying our house in 2020, I wanted to try using the self-adhesive wallpaper in my kitchen as a backsplash. After about 20 minutes of working with the wallpaper I began to get lightheaded and needed to step away from the project. I was struggling to think through some basic problems and had to ask my husband to help me. He ended up finishing the project for me so I could clear my head and stop a headache from coming on.

The issue was in the adhesive. Traditional wallpaper will have the same issue. Corn being used in adhesives is a long-standing tradition. I don't remember when I had to stop using Band-Aids because of the allergic response. I also cannot lick stamps or envelopes. Once again corn adhesive strikes! The key ingredient here is dextrin. It serves as the water-activated adhesive on stamps, envelopes, as well as wallpaper.

Completing The Hidden Consumer Journey

WE'VE COVERED a ton of examples in this book about the Hidden Consumer, who they are, and how your brand can reach them. Let's go over a few final points to remember for both companies and Hidden Consumers themselves.

FOR COMPANIES

If you are a company looking to increase revenue consistently here are a few takeaways to get you started:

- **Be transparent.** I know this is difficult due to the lack of knowledge of what is important and still needing to keep yourself safe, legally. But there are ways to achieve transparency without giving away your proprietary information. It starts with training your teams so that they understand people can be allergic to anything. The next step is for them to honestly say, "I don't know" if they cannot answer a question.

- **Vet your sources for ingredients.** If you don't know how your ingredients are made, you don't know what you are selling to the consumer. Understand how your ingredients are made by the manufacturer. I am giving everyone the benefit of the doubt by saying this is just a miscommunication error for all parties. This is also a different way to do business and discuss ingredients in products. However, your buyers want to know this information. As the adage goes, people only buy from those they know, like, and trust. In a $19B+ industry, you need to stand out as the safe option to as many people as possible.

- **Your website and customer service team are the keys to your success.** The website needs to have as much information about ingredients as possible. Your customer service teams need to be trained and educated in how to handle questions about ingredients and talk of allergies. If you rely on automated answers to questions your company is demonstrating ignorance. By not understanding the depth of intolerances and allergies you are demonstrating to consumers that you cannot be trusted. Allergy-Friendly shoppers are not shopping this way for fun. Usually someone's health or life is at stake if the wrong product is purchased.

At the end of the day, people with intolerances and allergies understand and share all the information they gather from your website and customer service. It's up to each company if they want to have a positive or a negative reputation. Remember, just because one person can't use your product doesn't mean someone else can't. In the intolerance and allergy communities we are always sharing brands that we use safely. But we are also sharing brands we cannot use but that have provided amazing customer service when we've called or written to ask questions of them.

For many companies, word of mouth marketing is key to their success. I am still learning about brands that are older than ten years. They never show up in search results because their websites do not accurately attract the person who is looking for their products. The other side of the coin is if websites were set up and designed with the ideal client and Hidden Consumer in mind, I would not have a business. I am happy to be a thought leader in this area and have a thriving business.

You need to think about the big picture and all departments that are impacted, train your staff on intolerances and allergies and what to say. We will create training information, update your database for training materials, if you use these tools. We can also train your staff on proper allergy responses and what needs to be considered. If you can be honest, they will trust you.

The goal is to see your customer's journey. How are they finding you, shopping for you, and buying your product? This will guide the strategy to reach as many points as possible. We work with your sales and marketing teams to see where they are today, where you want to go tomorrow, and develop the plan to get there.

Most importantly, all the ideal client language used on the website can be integrated into the big picture of your marketing strategy. Sales and marketing teams will be able to use specific language when selling directly to customers or when selling to store representatives.

Even though part of the focus of this book was on allergies, specifically mine, it does not mean we want more allergy-free or allergy-friendly products. We want to help businesses better explain their products to find their Hidden Consumers. You don't have to focus on allergies to be seen as allergy friendly. In most cases, putting anything "allergy" on your product label is a red flag for those who, like me, had to dig deeper to find safe products.

FOR CONSUMERS

If you are a Hidden Consumer, what you need to know is that companies cut costs anyway they can. The cheaper the ingredients the more likely you will find it in low-cost food. This means you must be more aware of how your ingredients are made, not just the food. Science is pointing to the more refined ingredients that are found in processed, ultra processed, and now bioengineered foods, which are more likely to damage your health. There are four things you can do to protect yourself and your family:

1. **Change your mindset.** Doctors and companies do not always have your best interest at heart. You must do your research or talk to people who have the information to understand how not to get sick.
2. **Educate yourself.** Every person's food sensitivity will react somewhat differently. You need to understand your body's limits. Don't depend on someone else to tell you what is safe. What is harmful to me probably won't be harmful to you. Only you can determine your level of tolerance. Be safe! There are many foods I don't eat because I don't know how bad the reaction will be.
3. **Find a food sensitivity support group around your intolerance or allergies.** It is a mood booster to know others are in the same boat and have navigated through the experience.
4. **Keep a food journal.** Track what you ate (with date and time), the ingredients in everything, and time and date of reactions. You will need this when you go see your doctor(s).

What is next? What can we do? From the standpoint of the environment, each person needs to start with looking at what plastics they can take out of their lives and replace them with stainless steel or glass. We need to go back to reusable items if we are going to drop some of our dependance on corn. I don't think it's a coincidence that the amount of plastic particles showing up in human stomachs and the number of plastics made from corn. Since our bodies cannot digest a corn kernel anyways, how do we expect it to digest a corn-based plastic?

What can we do from the perspective of our health? Look at the food you are eating and the amount of processed and ultra-processed food. Can you afford to move away from the convenience of cheap food? Many cannot. If you can't afford it, this will take a group effort. The issues around food are economic with people not being paid a living wage while shareholders make out like the bandits they are. The United States wastes a large amount of fresh food every single day. Can a system be put in place to help lower income families afford fresh fruit vegetables that are cost comparative to fast food?

At the end of the day, I want everyone to have the ability to make their own choices with the food they eat. If you are happy and content eating ultra-processed foods, you go be you and enjoy yourself. If you want to eat healthier, you should also have the option to do so. Our current standard is to hide the facts and pretend nothing is wrong. We will not be able to continue this ostrich with their head in the sand type of approach. The grass-roots approach to connecting brands and the Hidden Consumers they serve is a win-win for the businesses and consumers. Businesses who want to do better can confidently communicate the ingredients or materials in their products. Consumers can decide based on the facts for their health and safety. That is the outcome I want to support.

WRAPPING IT UP

There is always going to be a need for more research and more insights into how our effect on the environment impacts human life as well as our health. In some cases, more research is absolutely needed to determine what steps are needed to move us toward a healthier future. The problem is the amount of money spent to stop honest research from happening every day. We need to support the independent researchers and labs who work to bring well-rounded information to the public.

There are many reasons why so many adults are experiencing an onset of allergies late in life. From environmental pollution to overhanded use of specific ingredients in all aspects of our food industry, many factors are involved. Today, there are more children and adults who suffer food sensitivities than even 20 years ago.

I know there are many people who will shrug their shoulders and say, "It doesn't affect me, so I don't care." Here's the point: One day this may affect you or someone you love. It most definitely affects your Hidden Consumer customers. The research is showing that the food most Americans eat is killing them. Food from restaurants and the processed and ultra-processed "food" you buy in the store are all linked to severe health issues, both mental and physical. Research as recent as 2024 shows a growing trend in food that alters our DNA. Even the "healthy" food is processed in a way it is not completely safe to eat. Hidden Consumers should be allowed to make the choice of what they eat based on understanding the possible outcomes of their decision. As consumers, they deserve the ability to make their own choices. Brands must be ready to meet Hidden Consumers where they are to help make that happen.

Acknowledgements

THIS BOOK has been a thought for over a decade. As I went through my experiences of eliminating my intolerances and allergens, people wanted to learn more. The more I learned, the more people were shocked about what was really in our food. "You should write a book!" was an all-too-familiar statement. Thank you to Broad Book Group for working with me to get a book that I could be proud of and use to make a social impact.

My number-one cheerleader has always been my husband, **Lee**. Thank you for riding by my side throughout our journey together. My food intolerances and allergies and health always seem to push us beyond our comfort zones and yet we still come out on top. Everything we have accomplished would not have been possible without your support.

Tess Rollins, you have been supportive and willing to work with me through the ups and downs. Your support of the book and talking through obstacles we both experience due to marketing practices helped to better discuss the issues I can solve for companies. I am happy to have you as Hidden Consumers Consulting Branding Partner.

Betty and Jeff Luscher, both of you have shown what kindness really is. Your ability to jump in and prepare safe food for me and have amazing conversations is always a highlight in our weeks. No one else in my life has ever gone to the lengths you have to ensure I can eat as part of a group.

Vanessa and Jennifer, your guidance in this process of thought to a finalized book was top notch. I could not have asked for a better publishing team. You answered my questions and concerns and helped me understand the full process. Thank you for making this decade-long thought process a reality.

About The Author

AMY GRAVES is a passionate advocate for health-conscious consumers, a published author, and an expert in accessibility and inclusion. As the founder of Hidden Consumers Consulting, Amy helps brands in the natural and organic industries connect with the untapped and rapidly growing demographic of "hidden consumers"—individuals whose buying decisions are driven by health concerns, allergies, or sensitivities. Through strategic messaging, marketing, and automation, Amy empowers companies to attract, engage, and convert these consumers into loyal customers.

Amy's journey began with her own health challenges. For years, undiagnosed health issues pushed her to reexamine her relationship with food and products, sparking a deeper understanding of the overlooked challenges many consumers face. Her experience opened her eyes to the power of health-conscious buyers and inspired her mission to bridge the gap between brands and the consumers who need them most.

Amy is also a proud disability advocate. As a part-time wheelchair user and someone who has faced workplace discrimination, she transformed adversity into opportunity. After being repeatedly told she was a "risk" by potential employers, Amy chose to write her own story. She founded a successful business that employs others with disabilities, proving that inclusion isn't just possible—it's powerful. Learn more at **www.hiddenconsumersconsulting.com**.

References

1. "Food Allergy Consumer Journey." FoodAllergy.org, 2024. https://www.foodallergy.org/food-allergy-consumer-journey.

2. "The 14 Allergens." Food Safety Authority of Ireland, 2024. https://www.fsai.ie/business-advice/starting-a-food-business/allergens.

3. Youmshajekian, Lori. "How Do Ultraprocessed Foods Affect Your Health?" *Scientific American*, November 25, 2024. http://www.scientificamerican.com/article/how-do-ultraprocessed-foods-affect-your-health/.

4. Lane, Melissa M, Elizabeth Gamage, Shutong Du, Deborah N Ashtree, Amelia J McGuinness, Sarah Gauci, Phillip Baker, et al. "Ultra-Processed Food Exposure and Adverse Health Outcomes: Umbrella Review of Epidemiological Meta-Analyses." BMJ, February 28, 2024. https://doi.org/10.1136/bmj-2023-077310.

5. Food & Water Watch. "The Economic Cost of Food Monopolies: The Hog Bosses." Food & Water Watch, April 5, 2024. https://www.foodandwaterwatch.org/2022/05/05/food-monopolies-hog-factory-farms/.

6. "Chapter 3. Sources of Soil Pollution." Sources of soil pollution and major contaminants in agricultural areas, 2021. https://openknowledge.fao.org/server/api/core/bitstreams/fe5df8d6-6b19-4def-bdc6-62886d824574/content/src/html/chapter-03-3.html#:~:text=.%2C%202006).-,3.3.,Moncton%20Sewerage%20Commission%2C%202009).

7. "Chapter 3. Sources of Soil Pollution." Sources of soil pollution and major contaminants in agricultural areas, 2021. https://openknowledge.fao.org/server/api/core/bitstreams/fe5df8d6-6b19-4def-bdc6-62886d824574/content/src/html/chapter-03-3.html#:~:text=.%2C%202006).-,3.5.,Moncton%20Sewerage%20Commission%2C%202009).

8. "Animal Feed and Protein." Corn Refiners Association, March 21, 2025. https://corn.org/products/animal-feed-protein/.

9. Flesher, John. "Factory Farms Provide Abundant Food, but Environment Suffers." PBS, February 6, 2020. https://www.pbs.org/newshour/economy/factory-farms-provide-abundant-food-but-environment-suffers.

10. "Chapter 3. Sources of Soil Pollution." Sources of soil pollution and major contaminants in agricultural areas, 2021. https://openknowledge.fao.org/server/api/core/bitstreams/fe5df8d6-6b19-4def-bdc6-62886d824574/content/src/html/chapter-03-3.html.

11. Sajjad, Muhammad, Qing Huang, Sardar Khan, Muhammad Amjad Khan, Yin Liu, Junfeng Wang, Faqin Lian, Qingqing Wang, and Genmao Guo. "Microplastics in the Soil Environment: A Critical Review." *Environmental Technology & Innovation 27* (August 2022): 102408. https://doi.org/10.1016/j.eti.2022.102408.

12. "Chapter 3. Sources of Soil Pollution." Sources of soil pollution and major contaminants in agricultural areas, 2021. https://openknowledge.fao.org/server/api/core/bitstreams/fe5df8d6-6b19-4def-bdc6-62886d824574/content/src/html/chapter-03-3.html.

13. "Chapter 2. Main Soil Contaminants and Their Fate in the Soil Environment." Conclusions, 2021. https://openknowledge.fao.org/server/api/core/bitstreams/fe5df8d6-6b19-4def-bdc6-62886d824574/content/src/html/chapter-02-4.html.

14. Natalia;, PAYA PEREZ Ana; RODRIGUEZ EUGENIO. "Status of Local Soil Contamination in Europe: Revision of the Indicator 'Progress in the Management Contaminated Sites in Europe.'" JRC Publications Repository, January 1, 1970. https://publications.jrc.ec.europa.eu/repository/handle/JRC107508.

15. "Monsanto vs. U.S. Farmers." Center for Food Safety, 2005. https://www.centerforfoodsafety.org/files/cfsmonsantovsfarmerreport11305.pdf.

16. Food & Water Watch. "GMOs Plant Seeds for Corporate Control." Food & Water Watch, March 25, 2021. https://www.foodandwaterwatch.org/2021/03/02/gmos-plant-seeds-corporate-control/.

17. "Monsanto vs. U.S. Farmers." Center for Food Safety, 2005. https://www.centerforfoodsafety.org/files/cfsmonsantovsfarmerreport11305.pdf.

18. Spicer, Maggie. "Greenwashing Examples by Food and Drink Brands 2022-23: Provenance." RSS, 2023. https://www.provenance.org/news-insights/5-food-and-drink-brands-called-out-for-greenwashing-and-the-lessons-we-can-learn.

19. DAD, Tom Koch (Acting, and Stephanie T. Nguyen. "FTC Charges Companies with 'bamboo-Zling' Consumers with False Product Claims." Federal Trade Commission, May 29, 2009. https://www.ftc.gov/news-events/news/press-releases/2009/08/ftc-charges-companies-bamboo-zling-consumers-false-product-claims.

20. Program, Human Foods. "FY18-19 Sample Dairy-Free Dark Chocolate Products for Milk Allergen." U.S. Food and Drug Administration, March 5, 2024. https://www.fda.gov/food/sampling-protect-food-supply/fy1819-sample-collection-and-analysis-domestically-manufactured-dairy-free-dark-chocolate-products#:~:text=The%20agency%20found%20the%2012,101.65(b)(1).

21. Program, Human Foods. "Plant-Based Milk and Animal Food Alternatives." U.S. Food and Drug Administration, January 6, 2025. https://www.fda.gov/food/nutrition-food-labeling-and-critical-foods/plant-based-milk-and-animal-food-alternatives.

22. Program, Human Foods. "Questions and Answers on the Gluten-Free Food Labeling Final Rule." US Food and Drug Administration, 2024. https://www.fda.gov/food/nutrition-food-labeling-and-critical-foods/questions-and-answers-gluten-free-food-labeling-final-rule.

23. US Department of Agriculture, and Miles McEvoy National Organic Program Deputy Administrator. "Organic 101: What the USDA Organic Label Means." Blog, 2012. https://www.usda.gov/about-usda/news/blog/organic-101-what-usda-organic-label-means.

24. US Department of Agriculture Agricultural Marketing Service. "What Is a Bioengineered Food? ." 2021. https://www.ams.usda.gov/sites/default/files/media/BE_Consumer.pdf.

25. US Department of Agriculture. "USDA Launches Effort to Strengthen Substantiation of Animal-Raising Claims." Home, June 14, 2023. https://www.usda.gov/about-usda/news/press-releases/2023/06/14/usda-launches-effort-strengthen-substantiation-animal-raising-claims.

26. 26: "Letter from FDA Clarifies Natural Status of High Fructose Corn Syrup." IDFA, July 25, 2019. https://www.idfa.org/news/letter-from-fda-clarifies-natural-status-of-high-fructose-corn-syrup.

27. 27: "Sweeteners." Corn Refiners Association, March 21, 2025. https://corn.org/products/sweeteners/.

28. 28: "Sweeteners." Corn Refiners Association, March 21, 2025. https://corn.org/products/sweeteners/.

29. 29: Program, Human Foods. "Substances That Come in Contact with Food Information for Consumers." U.S. Food and Drug Administration, 2024. https://www.fda.gov/food/food-ingredients-packaging/food-packaging-other-substances-come-contact-food-information-consumers.

30. "The Environmental Impact of Corn-Based Plastics." *Scientific American*, February 20, 2024. https://www.scientificamerican.com/article/environmental-impact-of-corn-based-plastics/.

www.ingramcontent.com/pod-product-compliance
Lightning Source LLC
Chambersburg PA
CBHW052021030426
42335CB00026B/3231